SERIES ONE

BEGINNER/REFRESHER
BRIDGE

I LOVE BRIDGE
THE VALENTINE SERIES

SERIES ONE   **BEGINNER/REFRESHER BRIDGE**

SERIES TWO   **INTERMEDIATE BRIDGE**

SERIES THREE   **ADVANCED BRIDGE**

To purchase any of the above books
contact amazon.com
Search: I Love Bridge and the title of book
you want in the series
Questions: e-mail mimisbridgeclub@msn.com

Special thanks to my editor Barry Rigal for his insights and editing skills. Barry Rigal holds title to two North American Bridge Championships, is a Bridge commenter, journalist, and co-editor of the American Contract Bridge League's *Encyclopedia of Bridge*.

Table of Contents   *Look for Important Concepts in the Text!*

The origin of playing cards dates back to the year 979 A.D. in China where paper was invented. Card games such as triumph and ruff and honors were played primarily in England in the 16th century, and these games evolved into the card game whist, thought to mean "quiet", made famous by Edmond Hoyle's book, *"A Short Treatise on the Game of Whist,"* published in 1742.

Whist was introduced to the United States in 1690, and George Washington enjoyed playing whist and placed small wagers on the game.

Whist went through many stages of evolution in the following centuries. The English began playing duplicate whist in 1857. Duplicate whist was introduced to eliminate the "luck of the deal", as players would play the same hands and compare scores. Duplicate whist was introduced to the United States in 1880, and Americans began playing whist in duplicate club matches in 1883.

The game of Bridge evolved from whist. Early documentation notes that the name Bridge may have derived from the Russian term "biritch" which means players announce or herald their auction. In 1890, Bridge replaced whist in England and in the United States.

Harold S. Vanderbilt created a new method of scoring while playing Bridge on a cruise with friends and family through the Panama Canal in 1925. Thus Contract Bridge was born.

Ely Culbertson published best-selling books, *"The Culbertson Summary"* and the *"Blue Book,"* in 1931. In 1958, Charles Goren appeared on the cover of Time Magazine, and was named "The King of Aces." The Time article proclaimed Bridge as the worlds number one card game.

Bill Gates, Warren Buffet, Omar Sharif and Catherine Zeta Jones are some of the many celebrities playing Bridge today. President Eisenhower played Bridge regularly with top experts and attended national Bridge tournaments.

Bridge is considered an important exercise in maintaining intellectual alertness. The game is stimulating, competitive, and socially rewarding. Experienced players are continually learning new concepts, and there are thousands of books written on the subject of the game. Today, Bridge is played and enjoyed by many people worldwide.

INTRODUCTION

I began my Bridge teaching career in Marina del Rey, California in 2001, and moved to Palm Desert, California in 2008. In my new home in the desert, I found a wonderful community of people interested in learning Bridge, and others who wanted to update their Bridge game with the latest bidding systems.

Many of my students reside in the country clubs and senior retirement communities that dot the Coachella Valley in Southern California. I've taught Bridge classes at the Bighorn Golf Club, Indian Ridge, Tamarisk, Mountain View, Trilogy and Andalusia Country Clubs, and at the Segovia Retirement Community and La Quinta Wellness Center. I also teach small private groups. My husband and I direct sanctioned duplicate games at the Bighorn Golf Club, the Duncan Duplicate Bridge Club, and the Sun City Duplicate Bridge Club.

In 2008, I decided to write the *"I Love Bridge"* book series as a user-friendly approach to teaching the "nuts and bolts" of the game. I hope the books will be valuable as a teaching tool for Bridge teachers, and also function as a workbook for those interested in a self-learning textbook complete with sample hands and quizzes.

I believe students will continue to learn and improve their game if they are comfortable at the beginning of the learning process. This approach works well with my students, and they enjoy the easy-to-read text and practice hands that accompany each lesson.

I've taught the series to many students, and received positive feedback for the class material. After taking Beginning/Refresher classes, many students continue to learn Bridge by enrolling in my Intermediate and Advanced classes.

The *"I Love Bridge"* Beginner/Refresher book is designed for beginning Bridge players, and for those who have played in the past and want to update their game.

The Intermediate book introduces more complex elements of the game, and reinforces the "Framework of Bidding" point count rules. The book covers notrump responses such as Stayman, Jacoby transfers, Gerber, and quantitative bids. In addition there are chapters on preemptive bidding, balancing seat bids, negative doubles, takeout doubles, declarer play, reverse bidding, and the cross ruff among other topics.

The Advanced book offers many of today's popular conventions such as Lebensohl, Hamilton, control bids and declarer play, and includes the two-over-one game force bidding system.

Bridge is played throughout the world, and offers players exciting competitive events and social gatherings. One of my students was injured and unable to play golf and other sports. Bridge opened a new world of sociability and interest for him. The hugs of thanks from the student and his wife are very special to me, and one of the reasons I love teaching the game of Bridge. We learn, have fun, laugh and make new friends — what could be better?

BRIDGE CONDUCT AND ETIQUETTE

An awareness of the following rules is important so that the game is played fairly, making the game is enjoyable for you and your partner, and the opponents.

- Players should be courteous toward their partner and the opponents at all times.

- Place value on your Bridge partnership as you are working together as a team. Everyone makes mistakes, and there are decisions to be made in every hand. Respect your partner's decisions even if they turn out to be wrong for one particular Bridge hand.

- When you bid or make a call in Bridge, do not use special emphasis in your voice or body language to convey information.

- Do not use facial expressions to show displeasure or happiness at a bid, play or a lead by partner.

- Never try to deceive the opponents by taking more time than necessary in bidding or play of the hand. Try hard not to draw inferences from partner's hesitation in bidding or play.

- Play in a timely fashion, placing cards face up on the table. Do not detach a card before it's your turn to play. Don't snap the cards or play the cards in a way that might prevent players from seeing the card.

- Players should avoid any conduct or gratuitous comments that could embarrass their partner, the opponents, or interfere with the enjoyment of the game.

- Pay attention during the game.

- Always follow correct American Contract Bridge guidelines in all calls, bids and play of the hand during a Bridge game.

DEFINITIONS

AUCTION	Players bid to win the contract.
BID	Bid of a suit or notrump and a level from 1-7.
BOOK	The first six tricks taken by declarer.
BLACKWOOD	An ace and king asking convention.
CALL	A pass, double or redouble.
CONTRACT	Final bid followed by three passes.
DEAL	Deck of 52 cards dealt to all players clockwise around the table.
DECLARER	The person who plays the contract.
DEFENDERS	Opponents of declarer who try to defeat the contract.
DISCARD	Play of a card in another suit when you are out of the suit led.
DOUBLE	Call for take-out or penalty.
DUMMY	Partner of declarer.
DISTRIBUTION	The number of cards in each suit.
DOUBLETON	Holding only two cards in any suit.
FINESSE	Declarer play for a 50% chance of winning a trick depending on an opponent's holding in the suit.
FOLLOW SUIT	Players must follow to the suit led.
IDEAL FIT	At least eight-cards in any one suit held by the partnership.
LEAD	Opening lead to the first play, or first card led in subsequent plays.
LHO	Left hand opponent.
LOSER	A card that may lose a trick to the opponents.
MAJOR SUITS	Spades and Hearts.
MINOR SUITS	Diamonds and Clubs.
NOTRUMP	A contract played without trump
PENALTY DOUBLE	A call that increases the penalty for an unsuccessful contract
RESPONDER	Partner of opening bidder.
RHO	Right hand opponent.
RUFF	Using a trump card to win a trick.
SINGLETON	A holding of one card in a suit.
SLUFF	Discarding when void in a suit.
TRICK	Winner of 4-cards played.

 **NOTES**

 **CHAPTER ONE**

RANKING OF THE SUITS   *POINT COUNT*   *BRIDGE CONCEPTS*

Bridge is a partnership game. Always be courteous to your partner, as Bridge partnerships will only survive through mutual respect. Four players are needed to create a Bridge game. The dealer is the player who selects the highest card from the pre-dealt 52-card deck spread face down on the table. The dealer then proceeds to deal thirteen cards clockwise to each of the four players at the table.

- Players sit opposite their partners in seats designated as the four winds. North and South are partners and East and West are partners.

	NORTH	
WEST		EAST
	SOUTH	

Players should arrange their hands into suits by placing the suits from left to right.

Sample hand: Spade suit   Heart suit   Diamond suit   Club suit

♠AKJ102   ♥Q85   ♦J83   ♣54

- The first part of a Bridge game is a bidding auction, which proceeds clockwise around the table in which all four players participate. Each player in turn may pass, bid their best suit, or bid "notrump". A bid of notrump suggests there are a somewhat even number of cards in all four suits in the bidder's hand, referred to as a balanced hand.

- All bids use a special **"Framework of Bidding" Bridge language,** which you will learn in Chapters two, three and four. The partnerships compete with each other by bidding their suits or a notrump bid to try to win the auction, and the right to determine what the trump suit will be or if it's a notrump contract.

- **The contract is an agreement to fulfill the level of a suit or notrump bid by the partnership in the auction.** A level could be 1 through 7 of a suit or notrump. One person in the winning partnership is called the declarer and his partner is called the dummy. The losing partnership is called the defenders of the contract.

- **The second part of the game is the play of the contract by the declarer for the winning partnership.** Scoring the game is done after each contract has been played. Winning or losing points are noted on each partnership's score sheet. Scoring the game is found in Chapter Nine.

Bids are Made by Bidding the Major and Minor Suits.

The Major Suits

♠Spades
♥Hearts

The Minor Suits

♦Diamonds
♣Clubs

You may also Bid Notrump Instead of Bidding a Suit

 Ranking of the Suits and Notrump.

- **The game of Bridge ranks the suits and notrump in importance.** The ranking of the suits means you must bid **up one-level** if your suit follows a bid of a suit or notrump that is **higher-ranking** than the suit you want to bid.

- You may stay on the **same level** if your suit follows the bid of a suit that is a **lower-ranking** suit than the one you want to bid.

Highest in Rank - Notrump

Major Suits

Second in Rank - ♠ Spades
Third in Rank - ♥ Hearts

Minor Suits

Fourth in Rank - ♦ Diamonds
Fifth in Rank - ♣ Clubs

Bid the Suits Clockwise According to the Ranking of the Suits:

Example #1 **DEALER: NORTH BIDS 1♠**

↓

WEST BIDS 3 ♥ EAST BIDS 2 ♥
GO UP A LEVEL; ♥ LOWER THAN ♠ GO UP A LEVEL; ♥ LOWER ♠
↑

SOUTH BIDS 2 ♠ ←
SAME LEVEL; ♠ HIGHER THAN ♥

Example #2: **DEALER: NORTH BIDS 1♥**

↓

WEST BIDS 2♠ EAST BIDS 1♠
SAME LEVEL; ♠ HIGHER THAN ♥ SAME LEVEL; ♠ HIGHER THAN ♥
↑

SOUTH BIDS 2♥ ←
GO UP A LEVEL; ♥ LOWER THAN ♠

Bid the suits clockwise. What is the final contract followed by three passes.

#1 **DEALER: NORTH BIDS ___? ___♦**
→ PASS ↓
PASS

WEST BIDS ___? ___♥ EAST BIDS ___? ___♣
PASS EAST BIDS ___? ___♥
PASS

SOUTH BIDS___? ____♠ ←
PASS
PASS

What is the contract? _____ Who is the declarer? _____

11

#2   DEALER: NORTH - PASS
PASS
PASS

WEST BIDS __?___♥   EAST BIDS ___?___♥
PASS   PASS

SOUTH BIDS___?___♠
PASS
PASS

What is the contract? _____   Who is the declarer? _____

#3   DEALER: NORTH BIDS ___?___♣
PASS

WEST BIDS___?___♠   EAST BIDS ___?___♠
PASS   PASS

SOUTH BIDS___?___♣
PASS

What is the contract? _____   Who is the declarer? _____

#4   DEALER: NORTH ___?___♥
NORTH BIDS___?___♠
PASS

WEST BIDS ___?___♦   EAST BIDS ___?___♦
PASS   PASS

SOUTH BIDS___?___♠
SOUTH BIDS___?___♠
PASS

What is the contract? _____   Who is the declarer? _____

Answers to ranking the suits:

#1 North 1♦, East 2♣, South 2♠, West 3♥, North pass, East bids 4♥; All Pass- contract 4♥, West declarer
#2 North pass, East 1♥, South 1♠, West 2♥, North pass, All Pass- contract 2♥, East declarer
#3 North 1♣, East 1♠, South 2♣, West 2♠, All Pass- contract is 2♠, East declarer
#4 North 1♥, East 2♦, South 2♠, West 3♦, North 3♠, All Pass- contract is 3♠; South declarer

POINT COUNT

Honor cards are the ACE, KING, QUEEN, and JACK of each suit, and the honor cards have high card points (HCP) assigned to them. The ace is the highest card in the deck, followed by the king, queen and the jack in importance. The ace wins over the king, the king wins over the queen, and the queen wins over the jack.

Non-honor cards have no points assigned to them, and range in importance from the 10, 9, and 8, down to the 2 in each suit. Non-honor cards win according to their number such as a 9 wins over an 8, an 8 wins over a 7, etc.

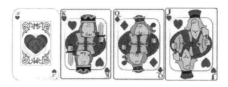

Count High Card Points (HCP) for Honor Cards

> Ace = 4 points
> King = 3 points
> Queen = 2 points
> Jack = 1 point

There are 40 high card points (HCP) in the deck.

> 4 aces = 16 points, 4 kings = 12 points
> 4 queens = 8 points, 4 jacks = 4 points
> Total = 40 HCP

Count Length Points: Long Suits are Always Good!

Add extra points for each card <u>over four cards</u> in a suit.

> five-card suit = one extra point
> six-card suit = two extra points
> seven-card suit = three extra points
> eight-card suit = four extra points
> nine-card suit = five extra points

**Always add both your HCP and your length points
to determine the total point count value of your hand.**

What is the point count for the hands below?   Answers for #3 - #10 on page 16.

Important: The 10 is <u>one</u> card – do not count the 10 as a 1 and 0 or 2 cards.
Remember to count an extra point for every card over four cards in a suit.

Examples: #1 and #2

#1

HAND A	POINTS	HAND B	POINTS	HAND C	POINTS
♠A109	4	♠75	0	♠A9632	4+1=5
♥KJ6342	4+2=6	♥KQJ7	6	♥AQ52	6
♦1076	0	♦AK652	7+1=8	♦954	0
♣10	0	♣86	0	♣8	0
TOTAL	10	TOTAL	14	TOTAL	11

#2

HAND A	POINTS	HAND B	POINTS	HAND C	POINTS
♠QJ42	3	♠AQ72	6	♠9632	0
♥A982	4	♥KQJ75	6+1=7	♥AQ52	6
♦AQ2	6	♦AK65	7	♦954	0
♣63	0	♣---	0	♣82	0
TOTAL	13	TOTAL	20	TOTAL	6

#3

HAND A	POINTS	HAND B	POINTS	HAND C	POINTS
♠10976		♠KQ87532		♠A10962	
♥KJ643		♥KQJ7		♥AJ52	
♦1076		♦10		♦954	
♣7		♣3		♣10	
TOTAL		TOTAL		TOTAL	

#4

HAND A	POINTS	HAND B	POINTS	HAND C	POINTS
♠J1074		♠7		♠J10642	
♥KQJ32		♥J62		♥KJ62	
♦1076		♦KQJ7		♦1076	
♣10		♣AQ1032		♣10	
TOTAL		TOTAL		TOTAL	

#5

HAND A	POINTS	HAND B	POINTS	HAND C	POINTS
♠J32		♠32		♠AJ7432	
♥QJ10		♥KJ2		♥KJ643	
♦A1076		♦AKQJ		♦107	
♣543		♣5432		♣---	
TOTAL		TOTAL		TOTAL	

#6

HAND A	POINTS	HAND B	POINTS	HAND C	POINTS
♠32		♠QJ10		♠KQ653	
♥KJ6432		♥32		♥653	
♦1076		♦KJ98		♦1076	
♣102		♣10987		♣J10	
TOTAL		TOTAL		TOTAL	

#7

HAND A	POINTS	HAND B	POINTS	HAND C	POINTS
♠AK98		♠KQ5		♠4	
♥2		♥J10987		♥KJ6432	
♦1076		♦AK1076		♦Q7654	
♣KQ1092		♣----		♣2	
TOTAL		TOTAL		TOTAL	

#8

HAND A	POINTS	HAND B	POINTS	HAND C	POINTS
♠A864		♠K109732		♠Q2	
♥A8765		♥3		♥KQ4	
♦		♦A6		♦A54	
♣9654		♣Q976		♣AK432	
TOTAL		TOTAL		TOTAL	

#9

HAND A	POINTS	HAND B	POINTS	HAND C	POINTS
♠A972		♠AQ97		♠4	
♥AQ8		♥AQ4		♥1086	
♦J109		♦Q6		♦AKJ103	
♣AK5		♣KJ104		♣A832	
TOTAL		TOTAL		TOTAL	

#10

HAND A	POINTS	HAND B	POINTS	HAND C	POINTS
♠K543		♠82		♠QJ1076	
♥AQ		♥K652		♥1043	
♦KQ84		♦A107		♦Q109	
♣K73		♣Q1096		♣A8	
TOTAL		TOTAL		TOTAL	

Answers to quiz on pages 14 and 15

#3

	Points		Points		Points
HAND A	5	HAND B	14	HAND C	10

#4

HAND A	8	HAND B	14	HAND C	6

#5

HAND A	8	HAND B	14	HAND C	12

#6

HAND A	6	HAND B	7	HAND C	7

#7

HAND A	13	HAND B	15	HAND C	9

#8

HAND A	9	HAND B	11	HAND C	19

#9

HAND A	18	HAND B	18	HAND C	13

#10

HAND A	17	HAND B	9	HAND C	10

BRIDGE CONCEPTS

SOLD TO THE HIGHEST BIDDER

The Auction:

- I'm sure everyone has experienced an auction. A Bridge auction is the calling of bids clockwise by each of the four players. In a Bridge auction, partnerships compete with each other to win the auction by bidding to win a certain number of "tricks".

  A trick is a set of four cards played clockwise by each of the four players, and won by one of the players. All players must follow a card from the same suit as the suit led. If you have no cards in the suit, you may throw a card from another suit, called a discard.

  Example: You play the ♠A followed by the ♠5, ♠10, and ♠J, each card played clockwise by the other three players. Your ♠A is the highest card and wins the trick. You have won one trick. If a player does not have a spade in his hand, he must play a card from another suit of his choice called a discard.

The Framework of Bidding Language:

- The game of Bridge is mathematically based, and just as music has a framework of scales and notes, the "Framework of Bidding" Bridge language will guide you in your bidding decisions.
- You will use the Bridge language to describe how many points and number of cards in a suit you have in your hand, and to assess the points in partner's hand by partner's use of the same Bridge language. Your points are similar to money used to bid in an auction. The more points you have, the higher you can afford to bid.

 ## The Final Contract:

When the remaining three players all pass consecutively, the last and highest suit or notrump bid becomes the final contract.

- When you win the number of tricks you've bid in the auction, you have successfully fulfilled the contract, and won a numbered score for your partnership. You don't want to bid more than your pair can afford to bid. If you bid too high and don't make the number of tricks you've bid, you've "gone down" in the contract, and the defense wins the numbered score.
- "Gone down" is a Bridge term used to mean you have not won the required tricks you bid in the contract.

♥ ♠
♣ ♦Trump Suit: A partnership wins the contract by making the final bid, and therefore can name the trump suit and the level where the contract will be played. In the auction below, dealer North opens the bidding 1♦, and the auction proceeds clockwise around the table.

	North (Dealer)	
	1♦	
West	Pass	East
2♥		1♥
		Pass
	South	
	1♠	
	Pass	

West's bid of 2♥ becomes the final contract when followed by three passes. Hearts are trump, and <u>East becomes declarer, as he was the first person to bid the trump suit.</u>

- The trump suit has special properties, and is similar to a "wild card" suit. A player must always follow a card to the suit led if possible. However, when a player is out of a suit, the player is "void" in that suit, and can choose to use a trump card to win the trick. You are not required to play a trump, and may decide to discard from another suit when you are void in the suit led. If more than one trump is played, the highest trump wins the trick. Example: A player leads the ♠A. You have no more spades and hearts are the trump suit. Your play of any heart will win the opponent's ♠A.

- Any player, including the defenders, can use the trump suit to win a trick when the player is void in the suit led. "Ruff" is the Bridge term used when you play trump to win an opponent's card. You have ruffed or trumped the trick. You can use a higher trump than an opponent's trump to "over-ruff" an opponent when both players are void in the suit led.

- As you are not required to play a trump card. You may decide to "sluff" or discard a card from another suit when you are void in a suit. Sluff is a Bridge term that means the discard of a non-trump card from another suit when void in the suit led. Of course, you don't want to trump high cards in partner's suit. If partner plays a winning card and you are void in the suit, you would merely discard a card from another suit.

Notrump Bid: You have a somewhat equal number of cards in the four suits. Your hand may be better suited to bid a notrump contract rather than a trump suit contract.

- In a notrump contract, only the highest card played in the suit led wins the trick. There is no trump suit to win tricks, and when you are void in a suit, you merely discard from another suit. Notrump tends to be bid with hands that do not have one suit that is significantly better or longer than the other three suits. Your hand may have high cards in most of the suits, and "balanced distribution", meaning an approximately equal number of cards in the four suits.

Opening Bidder:

- The dealer is the first person to have a chance to bid. If he does anything except pass he is defined as the opening bidder.

- The opener may pass, or bid a numbered level from 1-7 of a suit of ♠, ♥, ♦ or ♣ to begin the investigation as to whether that suit should be called the trump suit. You may also bid notrump, where no suit is named. If dealer passes the next player gets the same options as the opening bidder.

- The bids to make the correct number of tricks for the final contract is the most important aspect of the game, and should be a joint decision made by you and your partner.

Responder:

- The responder is the partner of the opening bidder for the partnership.

- The responder evaluates his hand after hearing partner's opening bid. Responder may agree with partner's suit (support him), bid another suit, bid notrump, or pass in response to partner's bid.

- The partnership can continue to make bids until they select a level from 1-7 in a trump suit or in a notrump contract. Both partners may also pass if they decide their combined points are not enough to win the contract over competitive bidding by the opponents.

- If all four players pass at their first turn to speak, the dealer will merely re-deal the hand.

Declarer:

- The declarer of the contract is the player who first bid a suit or notrump in the auction that becomes the final contract. This suit or notrump bid is the last and highest bid followed by three passes by the other players.

- Declarer plays both his hand and his partner's hand, called the dummy hand. Declarer will tell dummy what cards to play throughout the play of the hand.

- Either the opening bidder or his partner, the responder, may become the declarer in the contract.

 **Dummy:**

- Dummy is the partner of the declarer. After the left hand opponent (LHO) of declarer leads the first card, dummy tables his cards, and places dummy's suits in vertical rows facing declarer with the trump suit at dummy's right hand.

- Dummy has no input as to what cards to play, and must always follow instructions from declarer.

- When declarer shows out of a suit, dummy may ask declarer if declarer has no more cards in that suit. To prevent an infraction (i.e. a play from the wrong hand), dummy may remind declarer to play from the correct hand, as the lead to the next trick must always be played from the hand that won the prior trick.

 Play of the Hand:

- Play begins at the conclusion of the auction, and after the left hand opponent (LHO) of the declarer leads the first card. Players must always follow to the suit led by playing a card face up on the table, or discard from another suit if the player is void in the suit led. The player who wins the trick always leads to the next trick.

- It is good practice for declarer to take a moment to review both hands when the dummy is tabled. Before playing to the first trick, declarer decides on a plan of action to win the number of tricks the partnership bid in the auction.

- One plan may be for declarer to play high trump cards to draw or pull out all of the defender's trump cards so the defenders can't trump declarer's high cards. Dummy may hold another long strong "side" suit. A side suit is a suit other than the trump suit. Declarer may decide to first draw the defender's trumps, so that declarer can use his or dummy's long strong side suit to discard losing cards from his hand with no fear of the defenders trumping the side suit if they become void in the suit.

- **Declarer may instead decide to delay drawing defender's trumps.** Declarer may want first to trump losing cards in a suit from his hand if the dummy has a void in that suit.

- There are many strategies of declarer play in attempt to win the number of tricks bid in the contract. There are also defensive plays for the defenders who hope to defeat the contract and win points for their partnership. The endless combination of cards and strategies to win or defeat contracts contributes to the fascination of the game. As you progress in your knowledge of Bridge, you will learn how to plan the play of the hand as declarer effectively, and how to plan the defense of a contract as defenders.

<u>Bridge is a Game of Winning Tricks</u>:

Winning tricks: "Knocking out" opponent's high cards can win tricks by <u>promoting</u> lower honor cards in your suit.

Example: You have <u>KQJ</u>654. Leading the king can "knock out" an opponent's ace of the suit to promote your queen and jack to win tricks.

- You win tricks by trumping opponent's cards when you are **void** in their suits.
- You win tricks in a trump contract with the highest card of the suit led when all players follow suit, or when no one plays a trump.
- You win tricks with the highest card of the suit led in a notrump contract.
- You win tricks with low cards in long suits after the suit has been played a number of times. Playing high cards will draw the defenders cards in the suit, so that low cards may eventually win tricks, and is why we count length points in long suits. **Example: AKQJ<u>54</u>. After playing the AKQJ, the 54 should eventually win tricks.**

 Declarer must first make <u>BOOK or win SIX TRICKS</u>, before counting the number of tricks the partnership bid in the contract.

Book: The first <u>six tricks</u> taken by the declarer.
Example: You bid a contract of 4♠. You must make the first **<u>six tricks or book</u>**, plus the additional <u>four tricks</u> you bid in the auction in order to make your 4♠ contract. **You need a <u>total of 10 tricks</u>. Six book tricks + four bid tricks = 10 tricks**

Placement of Won or Lost Tricks: It's best to count your tricks "duplicate style". By placing the cards in front of you as suggested below, you can recreate the hand for review.

When you win the trick, place your card **VERTICALLY** in front of you.

When you lose the trick, place your card **HORIZONTALLY** in front of you.

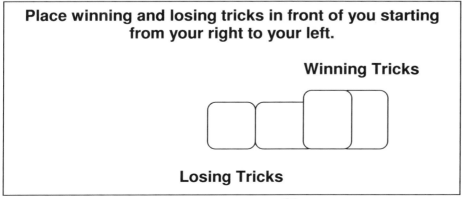

Place winning and losing tricks in front of you starting from your right to your left.

Winning Tricks

Losing Tricks

How many tricks do you need to make your bid?   Answers bottom of page

Reminder: You must first make "book" before counting your tricks.

1 Bid **3♠** = 9 tricks   2♠____?   4♠____?   6♥____?   6♠____?

#2   1♥____?   3♥____?   3♦____?   5♦____?   2♣____?

#3   1♠____?   4♣____?   3♣____?   5♣____?   7♠____?

#4   4♥____?   4♦____?   3NT____?   2NT____?   1NT____?

#5   6♣____?   1♣____?   5♥____?   6NT____?   7♣____?

#6   6♦____?   1♣____?   3♣____?   4NT____?   2♣____?

#7   5♥____?   7NT____?   5NT____?   2♥____?   7♦____?

  Answers:

#1	3♠=9	2♠=8	4♠=10	6♥=12	6♠=12
#2	1♥=7	3♥=9	3♦=9	5♦=11	2♣=8
#3	1♠=7	4♣=10	3♣=9	5♣=11	7♠=13
#4	4♥=10	4♦=10	3NT=9	2NT=8	1NT=7
#5	6♣=12	1♣=7	5♥=11	6NT=12	7♣=13
#6	6♦=12	1♣=7	3♣=9	4NT=10	2♣=8
#7	5♥=11	7NT=13	5NT=11	2♥=8	7♦=13

CHAPTER ONE
THE BOTTOM LINE

- Bridge is a partnership game with pairs North/South as partners and East/West as partners. Partnerships bid to determine which partnership wins the auction and names the contract.

- Count high card points (HCP): A=4 K= 3   Q = 2 J = 1 points.

- Add one extra point for every card over four cards in a suit. Always add your length points and your high card points to determine the opening value of your hand.

- If the final contract is at trumps, then any trump card will win out over the high cards in other suits as soon as a player is void or out of the suit led. A declarer or defender is not required to use a trump card when void in a suit, and may discard from another suit.

- You must follow suit to the card led. You can discard a card from another suit if you are void in the suit led, or use a trump card which to win the trick, provided you're not "over-trumped" by another player.

- Players may name a notrump contract, which means there is no named trump suit. If so, only the highest card in the suit led wins the trick.

- The player winning the trick leads to the next trick.

- The final contract is the last and highest bid followed by three passes.

Opening Bidder:

- The dealer is the first person to have a chance to bid. If he does anything except pass he is defined as the opening bidder.

Responder:

- The responder is the partner of the opening bidder.

Dummy:

- Dummy is the partner of the declarer. Opener or responder can become the declarer.

- After the left hand opponent (LHO) of declarer leads the first card, dummy tables his cards, and places dummy's suits in vertical rows facing declarer with the trump suit at dummy's right hand.

Notrump Contracts:

- You have a somewhat equal number of cards in the four suits. Your hand may be better suited to bid a notrump contract rather than a trump suit contract.

Suit Contracts:

- You and partner have found a good suit to name as the trump suit. The trump suit is like a "wild card" suit, which wins over the high cards in the opponent's suits when you are void in the suit led.

Play of the Hand:

- Play begins at the conclusion of the auction, and after the left hand opponent (LHO) of the declarer leads the first card. It is good practice for declarer to take a moment to review both hands when the dummy is tabled, and form a plan of action.

Bridge is a Game of Winning Tricks:

Winning tricks: "Knocking out" opponent's high cards can win tricks by <u>promoting</u> lower honor cards in your suit.

Declarer must first make <u>BOOK or win SIX TRICKS</u>, before counting the number of tricks the partnership bid in the contract.

The Contracts are in the following Suits or Notrump:

Notrump - Notrump Suit

Major Suits - ♠ and ♥

Minor Suits - ♦ and ♣

Players Must Bid According to the Ranking of the Suits and Notrump:

FIRST IN RANK - NOTRUMP
<u>MAJOR SUITS</u>
SECOND IN RANK - ♠ SPADES
THIRD IN RANK - ♥ HEARTS
<u>MINOR SUITS</u>
FOURTH IN RANK - ♦ DIAMONDS
FIFTH IN RANK - ♣ CLUBS

 **CHAPTER TWO**

FRAMEWORK OF BIDDING - PART ONE

EIGHT-CARD "IDEAL FIT"   OPENING VALUES AND RESPONSES

LEADS IN SUIT CONTRACTS

Why look for at least an eight-card "ideal fit" in the trump suit?

- There are thirteen cards of each suit in the deck.

- When you and partner hold at least 8+cards in a suit, your partnership has
the majority of cards in that suit, leaving the opponents with only five-cards in the suit.

   Why: The partnership needs at least an 8+card fit to provide declarer with enough
   trump cards to draw opponents' trumps, and also trump opponents' high cards
   in side suits.

- The 8+card suit fit is called the "ideal or golden fit" in a trump suit.

Opening Values: The + sign means "or more".

- The plus (+) sign means you may have more points in your hand or
cards in a suit when you bid.

- You must have at least a good <u>12+points</u> (HCP and length points)
to open the bidding called "opening values".

- In addition to opening values, you must have <u>five+cards in a major suit</u>
<u>to open the major at the one-level.</u>

- Therefore, when you open 1♠ or 1♥, you promise partner 12+points
and five+cards in a major suit you bid.

- If you have more than 12 points, your next bids called "rebids", will show
your higher point count or longer suits as the auction progresses.

- Holding opening values and five cards in any two suits, bid the
<u>higher-ranking suit</u> first, and bid the suits <u>down the line</u>.

   Example: Bid the spade suit first. ♠KQ1086   ♥AQ965

Responder:

- Responder must have at least <u>6+points</u> to respond to partner's opening bid, and usually passes with <u>0-5 points.</u>

- If opener bids 1♥ or 1♠, responder may raise partner's opening major to the two-level by bidding 2♥ or 2♠. The raise by responder promises <u>(6-10)</u> points, and at least <u>three+cards</u> in partner's opening major, and is called the <u>simple raise.</u>

- The simple raise promises no less than six points and no more than ten points, and <u>limits responder's upper point count to 10</u>. Since partner's opening bid must have at least five+cards in the major, responder's three+cards in the same major creates at least an eight-card fit in a suit.
  Example: 5+3 = 8. An "ideal fit" for a trump suit.

Opener <u>must</u> open with opening values, and may <u>not</u> hold a 5+card major.

- If so, opener may open the bidding with <u>three+cards in any minor suit.</u>
- Open 1♦ with four diamonds, and usually open 1♣ with equal 3-cards in the minors.

Responses to opener's 1♣ or 1♦ bid:

- When opener opens a minor, opener does not deny holding a <u>four-card major.</u>
- Therefore, responder should bid his 4+card major in response to opener's minor, as opener may have the same 4-card major as responder.
- If so, the partnership will find an 4-4 eight-card fit in the major to name as the trump suit.

Opener 1♣ or 1♦   Responder 1♥   Opener 2♥
Example: 4+4 = 8.   An "ideal fit" for a trump suit.

When opener bids a minor on the one-level, responder with <u>both four-card majors, bids the majors up-the-line, <u>or lowest ranking suit first.</u>

Bid hearts first holding: ♠AJ108 ♥J1076.

Why? Bidding the suits "up the line" keeps the bidding low and on the one-level, giving the partnership more bidding room to explore the final contract.

For example, when responder bids the heart suit first. Opener may <u>not</u> have 4-card heart support for responder's suit; however, opener can now rebid 1♠ with four spades. Opener only needs a 4-card suit for his spade rebid, or second chance to bid.
Example: Opener 1♣ or 1♦   Responder 1♥   Opener rebids 1♠   Responder also has 4-spades and supports opener's 1♠ bid by bidding 2♠.
The partnership has found a 4-4 = 8-card spade trump fit.

<u>Short Suits:</u> Zero, one or two cards in suits other than the trump suit. You can add extra points to your hand (short suit points) **ONLY** after you find an eight+card trump fit with partner.

> **Void = 0 cards in a suit**
> **Singleton = 1 card in a suit**
> **Doubleton = 2 cards in a suit**

We always count length points and HCP when we open our hand. However, <u>we do NOT add short suit points to our hand until we hear an agreement from partner of an ideal fit in our trump suit.</u>

Why: The partnership needs at least an eight+card fit to provide declarer with enough trump cards to draw opponents' trumps, and to trump opponents' cards in other side suits when <u>declarer or dummy is or becomes void in those side suits.</u> Both <u>opener and responder can re-evaluate their hands</u>, adding extra points for "short suits" when the partnership has found the eight+card fit in a suit. Short suits points are only counted in suit contracts.

For example: You bid 1♠ with 12 points, and partner bids 2♠. You've found at least an 8-card fit in spades. You have a void in hearts, and after hearing partner's support of your spade suit, you now add three points to your hand for the heart void. You've re-evaluated your hand to 15 points, but <u>not</u> <u>before</u> suit agreement with partner. You now have 15 points.
12 opening points + 3 points for the void = 15 points.

Extra Points for Short Suits

Declarer's short suit points:
    Singletons - 1 card in a suit = 2 points
    Doubletons - 2 cards in a suit = 1 point
    Void - 0 cards in a suit = 3 points

Responder or dummy's short suit points:
    Singletons - 1 card in a suit = 2 points
    Doubletons - 2 cards in a suit = 1 point
    Void - 0 cards in a suit is equal to the number of dummy's trumps.

Example: 3 trumps = 3 points; 4 trumps = 4 points; 5 trumps = 5 points, etc.

We add <u>void points</u> equal to responder's number of trumps, as responder may be the dummy, with the "<u>short side</u>" of the trump suit. Trumping on the "short" side of the trump suit could provide extra tricks for declarer. Example: Spades are trump.

♠AKQ107 ♥432   Dummy ♠ <u>9864</u> ♥0
Long side of trumps   Short side of trumps
Trump three losing hearts in dummy's heart void – three extra tricks for declarer.

Why are we counting points?

It is important to understand approximately how many combined partnership points are needed to bid the following game and slam contracts. It's also important to recognize that a responder's opening hand facing partner's opening hand should produce a game contract.

Suggested combined partnership points needed for games and slams.

Games and Slams		Suggested Points Needed
Notrump Game:	3NT	25 - 26 points
Major Suit Game:	4♠/4♥	25 - 26 points
Minor Suit Game:	5♦/5♣	28 - 29 points
Small Slam:	6NT/6♠/6♥/6♦/6♣	33 - 36 points
Grand Slam:	7NT/7♠/7♥/7♦/7♣	37 - 40 points

You must bid and make your games or slams to receive extra bonus points.
More about scoring the game in Chapter 9.

Bonus Points:

- You make extra bonus points when you bid a game or slam contract.
  Game contract: 3NT, 4♠, 4♥, 5♦, 5♣
  Small slam contracts: 6NT, 6♠, 6♥, 6♦, 6♣
  Grand slam contracts: 7NT, 7♠, 7♥, 7♦, 7♣

Part Scores: Any contract that isn't a game or slam is defined as a part score.

- Many hands do not have the combined partnership points to make games or slams. You can end the auction in a **part score** when the partnership determines there are not enough partnership points for those contracts. Part scores receive fewer bonus points than game or slam contracts.
- **Your side may make more tricks than you bid. However, you don't receive game or slam bonus points unless you actually bid game or slam.**
  Example: You bid 3♠ and made 4♠. You will receive points per each trick and points for the part score, however no extra game bonus points unless you actually bid the 4♠ game.
- **Part scores are: 1, 2, or 3-levels in a major suit contract. 1, 2, 3, or 4-levels in a minor suit contract 1 or 2-levels in a notrump contract.**

How many suggested partnership points are needed for the contracts?
Answers at bottom of page.

#1   3NT_____ ; 6NT_____ ; 4♥_____ ; 4♠_____ ;

#2   5♣ _____ ; 5♦_____ ; 7♦_____ ; 6♣_____ ;

#3   6♠_____ ; 7♠_____ ; 7NT_____ ; 6♦_____ ;

#4   6♥_____ ; 7♥_____ ; 7♣_____ ; 7♠_____ ;

Which contracts are part scores, games, small or grand slams?

#5   2NT_____ ; 3NT_____ ; 3♥_____ ; 4♠_____ ;

#6   4♣_____ ; 5♦_____ ; 7♦_____ ; 3♣_____ ;

#7   3♠_____ ; 7♠_____ ; 4NT_____ ; 4♦_____ ;

#8   4♥_____ ; 6♥_____ ; 1NT_____ ; 6NT_____ .

 How many points are needed to make the following contracts?

#1	3NT 25-26	6NT 33-36	4♥ 25-26	4♠ 25-26
#2	5♣ 28-29	5♦ 28-29	7♦ 37-40	6♣ 33-36
#3	6♠ 33-36	7♠ 37-40	7NT 37-40	6♦ 33-36
#4	6♥ 33-36	7♥ 37-40	7♣ 37-40	7♠ 37-40

Which contracts are part scores, games or slams?

#5	2NT part score	3NT game	3♥ part score	4♠ game
#6	4♣ part score	5♦ game	7♦ grand slam	3♣ part score
#7	3♠ part score	7♠ grand slam	4NT game and over trick	4♦ part score
#8	4♥ game	6♥ small slam	1NT part score	6NT small slam

Distribution: Distribution is the number of cards in each suit in your hand.

Balanced distribution:

- Balanced distribution is also called a **"flat"** hand, as the cards are distributed somewhat equally, such as 3-3-3-4, 3-2-4-4, and 5-3-3-2 in the suits.
- No voids, no singletons, and in some cases only one doubleton. There is little **ruffing or trumping value** in a balanced hand with few short suits.
- This type of hand may well play better in a notrump contract.

Example of a balanced hand: ♠AQ7, ♥1075, ♦KQ98, ♣Q102

Unbalanced distribution:

- We usually prefer **"unbalanced"** hands in suit contracts due to the ruffing values in the short suits of the hand.
- Ruffing values means we can use our trump to ruff opponent's high cards when we are void in a suit. The example hand below has a singleton heart and a doubleton club.

Example of an unbalanced hand: ♠AK985, ♥2, ♦KJ752, ♣72.

The point count rules and concepts in the Framework of Bidding are guides to help your partnership accurately arrive at successful contracts.

QUIZ: Answers are found on page 35.

As opener, you should ask yourself these questions.

1. What has responder's told me by his a simple raise i.e 1♠ opener - 2♠ responder.
2. What has responder told me when he passed at his first chance to bid?
3. I have two five card suits. How should I bid the suits?
4. I have 12 points. How should I decide if I should open the bidding.

As responder, you should ask yourself these questions.

5. What did partner promise when he opened 1♠ or 1♥?
6. Partner opened a 1♣ or 1♦. I have two four-card majors. How should I bid the suits?
7. I have 6 points and must bid. I can't support partner's suit, and I don't have a good suit of my own. What is my bid?
8. When can I re-evaluate my hand and add points for short side suits in my hand?

Quick Tricks: Does your opening hand have at least 2½ quick tricks?

- We need a <u>good</u> 12+points to open the bidding. Quick tricks (QT) help us determine if our 12 points are good enough to open. Of course, all 13+points must be opened.

- Quick Tricks are aces, kings with queens in the same suit, aces with queens in the same suit, and kings with small cards.

- Counting quick tricks is another guide to evaluate your opening values. You should open the bidding holding at least 2½ quick tricks.

- <u>Do not</u> add additional points for quick tricks. The quick trick count is used only as a check on your opening values.

- Queens and jacks standing alone or together are not quick tricks and are called slow tricks. Holding too many of your points in queens and jacks detract from the value of your hand. However, there is more value with those holdings when kings, aces and **tens** accompany them.

    Example: ♠QJ9, ♥QJ54, ♦<u>K9</u>, ♣QJ83. Although this hand has 12 HCP, the hand may not hold good opening values with only the **♦ K9 as a ½ quick trick**. Also, the distribution is balanced with the points scattered throughout the suits, offering little ruffing value.

Quick Trick Count

AK = 2 QT
AQ = 1 & ½ QT
A = 1 QT
KQ = 1 QT
Kx = ½ QT

Hand A - Open 1♥ (five-card major)		Hand B - Open 1♣ (no five-card major)	
♠9	0	♠AK102	2
♥AQ1085	1 and 1/2	♥K974	1/2
♦KQ109	1	♦54	0
♣987	0	♣Q107	0
	2 1/2 QT		2 1/2 QT

What is your opening bid or is it a pass?

♠AK1098	♠876	♠AKJ
♥QJ1098	♥A87	♥10754
♦J8	♦AQJ	♦AQJ43
♣2	♣10987	♣4
Points 13; Bid 1♠	**Points 11; Bid pass**	**Points 16; Bid 1♦**

#1

♠K43	♠Q42	♠AQ108
♥QJ1098	♥92	♥43
♦8765	♦AK43	♦AQ
♣2	♣J965	♣Q9432
Points____; Bid____	Points____; Bid____	Points____; Bid____

#2

♠AK1092	♠A9632	♠J1098
♥J1094	♥K7	♥QJ109
♦53	♦KQ72	♦AQJ
♣A2	♣62	♣43
Points ____; Bid____	Points____; Bid____	Points____; Bid____

#3

♠KJ9543	♠AQ3	♠J1098
♥QJ2	♥QJ7642	♥AKJ4
♦---	♦AQ32	♦AQJ4
♣AKJ9	♣---	♣10
Points____; Bid____	Points____; Bid____	Points____; Bid____

#4

♠A2	♠A9732	♠QJ10987
♥KQ	♥KQ975	♥QJ9
♦J432	♦AQ	♦A3
♣KQ762	♣8	♣KQ
Points____; Bid____	Points____; Bid____	Points____; Bid____

#5

♠Q9	♠109	♠654
♥K1065	♥J10	♥1098
♦AQ54	♦AQJ	♦AQJ
♣K98	♣AKJ1098	♣K1098
Points____; Bid____	Points____; Bid____	Points____; Bid____

Answers:

#1 7 points, pass	10 points, pass	15 points, bid 1♣
#2 13 points, bid 1♠	13 points, Bid 1♠	11 points, pass
#3 17 points, bid 1♠	17 points, Bid 1♥	16 points, bid 1♦
#4 16 points, bid 1♣	17 points, Bid 1♠	17 points, bid 1♠
#5 14 points, bid 1♦	18 points, Bid 1♣	10 points, pass

OPENING LEADS IN SUIT CONTRACTS: When you are defending, you get to fire the first shot by your opening lead. Choosing the opening lead is one of the more difficult parts of the game. Listed below are possibilities you can consider when leading to the first trick against an opponent's contract.

Lead top of a sequence: A sequence is two or more cards in a <u>contiguous sequence</u>. When you lead top of a sequence you hope to set-up winners for your side before declarer can get rid of his losers. Or you want to **"knock out"** an opponent's higher card in the suit, and promote your honor in the suit. **Example:** <u>A</u>Kxxx <u>K</u>Qxx <u>J</u>1076 <u>Q</u>J43
Lead from an interior sequence: Defined as a sequence with a non-touching honor.
Example: Lead the jack from KJ1098, or a broken interior sequence KJ986.

Lead low from an honor: Leading a low card tends to show you may have an honor in the suit. You can signal your partner you may have a <u>high card in a suit by leading a low card in the suit.</u> For example, leading low from a king may be a good lead, as only the ace is higher and your partner may have the queen to force out opponent's ace.

Lead "top of nothing": Spot cards are the 10 down to the 2. Leading a high "spot" card usually denies an honor in the suit. **You can signal you have <u>nothing in a suit by leading a high card in the suit.</u>** A lead of a **top of nothing** card does not necessarily show a doubleton. However, don't lead the 10 from e.g. 1063; lead low.

Standard leads and count: When you have <u>not</u> supported partner's suit, lead the top card of a doubleton. **Example of top of a doubleton:** <u>9</u>8 <u>5</u>3 <u>8</u>6

However as an exception, lead the king first from A<u>K</u> with a doubleton in partner's suit. The lead of the king then the ace shows the AK doubleton.

Why? When you lead a doubleton partner's suit, the high-low "signals" partner you have two cards in the suit. You hope to be able to trump the third round of the suit. **When partner has not bid the suit, be wary of making the doubleton lead -- especially from an honor, as the lead may help the opponents set up their long suit.**

Leads in partner's supported suit: Lead low from three or four cards to an honor in the suit, or with no honor in the suit, lead your highest card. Since you have supported the suit, the lead will not be a confused with a doubleton.

Example: K7<u>2</u> low from an honor   <u>8</u>764 top of nothing

Lead singletons: Lead singletons other than in the trump suit.

Why? The singleton lead may be in an opponent's side suit or partner's suit. You hope to trump an opponent's high cards, or partner's low cards in that side suit, once you become void in the suit. Leading a singleton in the opponent's trump suit, however, may finesse partner's high trump card, as declarer is last to play to the trick, and declarer may have a higher honor to capture partner's honor card. **Example: top of nothing leads - <u>8</u>65, 7632**

Don't lead away from A or AQ in a suit contract.

A and AQ are generally used to capture kings. Try <u>not</u> to lead away from <u>unsupported</u> Aces or AQ <u>unless partner has bid the suit.</u> The Q is not contiguous and therefore does not support the K.
Example: An unsupported Ace - Axxx. Not a good lead unless partner has bid the suit.
Lead A from <u>A</u>Kxx. The ace is a good lead as the <u>king supports the ace.</u>

Why? If you lead away from an A or AQ, declarer may have a singleton in the suit, and will trump your A when the suit is next played. Also, if your A or AQ is located to declarer's left, your K or AQ may be poised to capture declarer's king.

What do you lead in a suit contract?   Answers bottom of page.

♥QJ3_____   ♥J1062_____

♠KQ86_____   ♠7643_____

♠AKQ86_____   ♦98 (partner's suit)_____

♥Q654_____   ♠AQ87_____

♠QJ109_____   ♠65_____

♠QJ1083_____   ♦K543_____

♥A752_____   ♥KJ982_____

♠KJ1086_____   ♠J875_____

♠K92_____   ♦J2 (partner's suit)_____

♣2_____   ♣8754_____

Answers:

♥**Q**J3   top of a sequence
♠**K**Q86   top of a sequence
♠**A**KQ86 top of a sequence
♥Q65**4**   low from an honor
♠**Q**J109   top of a sequence
♠**Q**J1083 top of a sequence
♥A752   don't lead suit unless bid by partner
♠K**J**1086 top of interior sequence
♠K9**2**   low from an honor
♣**2**   lead singleton unless trump

Leads in Suit Contracts

♥**J**1062   top of a sequence
♠**7**643   top of nothing
♦**9**8   partner's suit (high/low doubleton)
♠AQ87   don't lead suit unless bid by partner
♠65   usually don't lead unless bid by partner
♦K54**3**   low from an honor
♥K**J**982   top of an interior broken sequence
♠J87**5**   low from an honor (need 4 in the suit)
♦**J**2   partner's suit (high/low doubleton)
♣**8**754   top of nothing

CHAPTER TWO - THE BOTTOM LINE

Opening Values.

Always count HCP and length points when you open the bidding. You should have a good 12+points to open the bidding.

Add short suit points <u>only</u> after you have found an "ideal" eight+card fit in a suit.

Opener:
- With opening values, you need at least five+cards in a major suit to open one of a major, or you may open a three+card minor if you have no five-card major.
- Open 1♦ with four diamonds, and usually open 1♣ with equal 3-cards in the minors.
- Holding opening values and five cards in any two suits, bid the <u>higher-ranking suit</u> first, and bid the suits <u>down the line</u>.

Responder:
- Responder needs at least <u>6+points</u> to respond to partner's opening bid.
- Responder usually passes with <u>0-5 points.</u>
- Responder needs (6-10) points and three+cards in partner's major suit to raise the major at the two-level, called the **SIMPLE RAISE.**
- Responder's bid of a <u>new suit</u> at the <u>one-level</u> shows at least 6+points, and at least four+cards in the suit.
- Responder's bid of a <u>new suit</u> at the <u>two-level</u> shows at least <u>10+points</u> and at least <u>four+cards in any minor suit.</u>
- Over a 1♠ opening bid, a 2♥ response shows at least <u>10+points</u> and at least <u>five+cards in the heart suit.</u>
- Respond in your four+card major to opener's minor suit bid.
- Responder holding both four-card majors, bids the <u>lower-ranking suit</u> first,
- and bids the major suits <u>up-the-line.</u>

<u>Opener's answers to the quiz on page 30.</u>

1. Responder has (6-10) points and at least 3 cards in my suit.
2. Responder does not have a good 12 points to open the bidding.
3. I must bid my 5-5 card suits down the line, higher ranking suit first.
4. I should check my quick tricks to see if I have 2 ½ quick tricks to open.

<u>Responder, you should ask yourself these questions</u>.

5. My partner promised at least a good 12+points and at least 5 cards in the major suit when partner opened the bidding.
6. When partner opens a minor suit, I should bid my four card major suits "up-the-line". Partner could have a four-card major suit.
7. I can bid 1NT with 6 points and no suit to bid on the one-level.
9. I can add short points only when the partnership has found an 8+card fit.

Suggested Partnership Points Needed for Games and Slams:

It is important to understand approximately how many combined partnership points are needed to bid the following game and slam contracts. It's also important to recognize that a responder's opening hand facing partner's opening hand may produce game.

Games		Suggested Points Needed
Notrump Game:	3NT	25 - 26 points
Major Suit Game:	4♠/4♥	25 - 26 points
Minor Suit Game:	5♦/5♣	28 - 29 points
Small Slam:	6NT/6♠/6♥/6♦/6♣	33 - 36 points
Grand Slam:	7NT/7♠/7♥/7♦/7♣	37 - 40 points

Part Scores: Many combined hands don't have the required points to make game or slam contracts. When you do not have the combined partnership points for games, you can end the auction in a part score as follows:
- 1, 2, or 3-level in a major suit contract
- 1, 2, 3, or 4-level in a minor suit contract
- 1 or 2-level in a notrump contract.

Do you have 2 ½ quick tricks (QT) to open the bidding?

> **AK = 2 QT**
> **AQ = 1 ½ QT**
> **A = 1 QT**
> **KQ – 1 QT**
> **Kx = ½ QT**

Leads in suit contracts:

- Lead top of a sequence. Example: <u>K</u>Qx.
- When you've supported partner, lead low from an honor.
- Lead the top card of a doubleton, usually if partner has bid the suit.
- Lead singletons other than the trump suit.
- Lead low from an honor such as K<u>x</u>x, except from the A or AQ. In that case, you should avoid leading the suit when partner has not bid the suit.

#1

North
♠965
♥QJ98
♦10986
♣A3

West
♠J84
♥A1054
♦AJ
♣9865

East
♠Q72
♥K76
♦K72
♣QJ102

South (Dealer)
♠AK1043
♥32
♦Q54
♣K74

South is the dealer with _____points and bids_____; West passes; North with _____points bids_____; All Pass. What is the contract_____? Who is the declarer_____? Who leads the first card_____? What is the lead___?

#2

North
♠543
♥AK86
♦J5
♣K762

West
♠KQ10
♥J109
♦Q97
♣9854

East (Dealer)
♠A8762
♥53
♦K1043
♣A3

South
♠J9
♥Q742
♦A862
♣QJ10

East is the dealer with _____points and bids_____; South passes; West with _____points bids_____; All Pass. What is the contract_____? Who is the declarer_____?
Who leads the first card_____? What is the lead___?

#3

North
♠A9
♥A76
♦Q654
♣9632

West (Dealer)
♠8742
♥104
♦KJ8
♣AKQ8

East
♠KQ106
♥K82
♦10732
♣105

South
♠J53
♥QJ953
♦A9
♣J74

West is the dealer with _____points and bids_____; North passes; East with _____points bids_____; South passes; West bids_____; All Pass. What is the contract_____? Who is the declarer_____? Who leads the first card_____? What is the lead___?

#4

North (Dealer)
♠109
♥AQ74
♦AQ32
♣Q96

West
♠AK63
♥5
♦954
♣K5432

East
♠QJ5
♥9832
♦KJ7
♣1087

South
♠8742
♥KJ106
♦1086
♣AJ

North is the dealer with _____points and bids_____; East passes; South with _____points bids_____; West passes; North bids _____; All Pass. What is the contract_____? Who is the declarer_____? Who leads the first card_____? What is the lead___?

Answers to practice hands pages 37-38.

#1

South is the dealer with 13 points and bids 1♠; West passes; North with 8 points bids 2♠. All Pass. What is the contract? 2♠. Who is the declarer? South. Who leads the first card? West. What is the lead? ♣9 - top of nothing lead.

- **West does not want to lead away from the ♥A or ♦AQ, and leads the ♣9.**

- **North knows partner's opening spade bid promises at least five spades. North bids 2♠ holding three spades and 6-10 points, called the "simple raise". North has upgraded his hand one point holding the doubleton club with the spade fit.**

- **After hearing partner's spade support, South also upgrades his hand one extra point for the doubleton heart to 14 points.**

- **South's 14 points plus North's upper limit of 10 points for the simple raise equals only a possible 24 points.**

- **The partnership does not have the 25-26 points needed to bid the 4♠ game.**

- **South passes.**

#2

East is the dealer with 12 points and bids 1♠; South passes; West with 8 points bids 2♠, the simple raise. All Pass. What is the contract? 2♠. Who is the declarer? East. Who leads the first card? South. What is the lead? ♣Q - top of a sequence lead.

- **After hearing spade support from partner, East upgrades his hand two extra points to 14 points, holding the heart and club doubletons.**

- **East's 14 points plus West's upper limit of 10 points for his simple raise equals only a possible 24 points.**

- **The partnership does not have the 25-26 points needed to bid the 4♠ game.**

- **East passes.**

#3

West is the dealer with 13 points and bids 1♣; North passes; East with 8 points bids 1♠;
South passes; West bids 2♠; All Pass.
What is the contract? 2♠. Who is the declarer? East. Who leads the first card? South.
What is the lead? ♥Q - top of a sequence lead.

- **West opens 1♣ holding no five-card major.**

- **East responds 1♠ (must have at least four cards in the suit).**

- **West knows East has at least four cards in the spade suit, and with his four spades, knows there is an eight-card spade fit. West bids 2♠.**

- **East can upgrades his hand to nine points with the doubleton club after hearing there is a spade fit with partner. However, West's 2♠ rebid limits his hand to no more than 15 points – not enough for game. 15+9=24 points.**

- **Game in a major suit is 25-26 so East passes.**

#4

North is the dealer with 14 points and bids 1♦; East passes; South with 9 points bids 1♥;
West passes; North bids 2♥; All Pass.
What is the contract? 2♥. Who is the declarer? South. Who leads the first card? West:
What is the lead? ♠A - ace from ace-king is a good lead.

- **North opens the bidding 1♦ holding no five-card major.**

- **South bids the lower ranking heart suit first, holding both four-card majors.**

- **North knows there is now an eight-card fit in the heart suit and bids 2♥.**

- **South passes as North's 2♥ rebid has limited his hand.**

 **CHAPTER THREE**

FRAMEWORK OF BIDDING - PART TWO

REBIDS   FORCING AND NON-FORCING BIDS   THE FINESSE

Concepts are repeated as we add to the Framework of Bidding.

Opener's first bids:

- To open the bidding, you must have "opening values" of a good 12+points (HCP and length points).

- If you have more points, your rebids will show your higher point count as the auction progresses.

Responder's first bids:

- Responder must bid with 6+points. Pass with 0-5 points.

- Responder may raise partner's opening suit to the two-level with (6-10) points and 3+cards in the suit - called the SIMPLE RAISE. 1♠ - 2♠

- Responder may jump raise partner's opening suit to the three-level with (10-12) points and 3+cards in the suit - called the LIMIT RAISE. 1♠ - 3♠

- Responder may bid 1NT with (6-10) points and no 4-card major and no support for partner's major suit.

- Responder may bid a new suit with 6+points and four+cards in the suit at the one-level. 1♥ - 1♠

- Responder needs 10+points to bid a new suit at the two-level. 1♥ - 2♣

- Responder needs 10+points, and at least four+cards in a minor to bid the minor suit at the two-level. 1♦ - 2♣.

- However, responder must have five+cards and 10+points in the heart suit to bid 2♥ over a 1♠ opening bid. 1♠ - 2♥

Rebids: A rebid is defined as subsequent calls by either opener or responder.

- This is the main opportunity for either player to limit the strength of their hand by their rebids.

- Rebids by opener and responder require judgment based on the number of points and distribution of cards in their hands.

- By continuing to add the combined partnership points, the partnership will decide what level and strain of a suit or notrump will be the successful **contract.**

 **Don't rebid a 5-card suit when partner has not supported the suit.**

- Your rebid of the suit shows a six+card suit, and partner may support you with only two cards in the suit.

  Example:

Opener	Responder
1♠ AJ10876 ♥AJ4 ♦K72 ♣ 87	2♣ ♠Q8 ♥QJ3 ♦1076 ♣AK1065
2♠	4♠

Opener's rebid of the spade suit shows a 6+card suit, and responder with two spades can now support the suit and bid game. 6+2 = 8 card fit.
In this case, opener with opening values + responder with opening values should produce game.

- Opener with 5-5 distribution in any two suits, bids the higher-ranking suit first, and bids the suits <u>down-the-line.</u>

  Example: Bid the diamond suit first. ♦QJ1087 ♣KQJ98

However, you can rebid a 5-card suit to show 5-5 in the two suits.

Opener	Responder
1♠ ♠AKJ86 ♥QJ1076 ♦87 ♣9	2♣ ♠Q8 ♥A87 ♦J5 ♣AK7652
2♥	3♣
3♥	4♥

- In the above auction, opener has shown 5-5 distribution in the major suits by bidding and then rebdding the heart suit. Opener bids his heart suit on his second chance to bid in this type of holding. <u>5-4+</u> cards in the majors.
- Responder can't support opener's heart suit initially, as it may be only a 4-card suit.
- However, now that opener has <u>rebid </u>his heart suit showing five hearts, responder can support partner's heart suit with his <u>3-card suit.</u> 5+3 = 8 card suit.

 **FORCING AND NON-FORCING BIDS:**

When a player has <u>never passed</u> in the auction, the player is called a
(NPH) non-passed hand, and therefore has an <u>unlimited</u> point count.

When a player initially <u>passes</u> at his first chance to bid, and now responds to his
partner, the player is called a passed hand (PH) responder, and by pass, has
<u>limited</u> his point count to less than good opening values.

Non-Passed Hand Responder:

When a NPH responder bids a <u>new suit</u>, responder's bid <u>forces</u> opener to bid
again for at least one more round of bidding. The (+) sign indicates responder has
an un-limited upper point count in his hand.
Example: 6+points or 10+points.

- The <u>forcing</u> bid gives opener an opportunity to further describe his hand.
- A NPH responder does not have to jump at his first bid to show a strong hand.
  If responder jumps, his bid may crowd opener's bidding space, and not allow
  opener to jump to show his point count.
- After responder's forcing bid, responder will further describe the strength
  of his hand in his rebids.
- Responder's <u>new suit</u> at the one-level shows <u>6+points and 4+cards</u> in the suit.
- Responder's <u>new suit</u> at the two-level shows <u>10+points and 4+cards in any</u>
  <u>minor suit,</u> or <u>10+points and five+cards in the heart suit over a 1♠ bid.</u>

Passed Hand Responder:

When a player <u>passes</u> at his first chance to bid in the auction, the player is called a passed
hand (PH) responder. Any time responder <u>limits</u> his hand, his bids are <u>non-forcing</u>.
Opener may pass if opener determines the partnership does not have enough points for
a game or slam contract.

A PH responder has <u>limited</u> his hand to <u>no more than 11 points</u> by his initial pass.
- Opener may choose to bid or pass.
- Responder's support of partner's suit or notrump bids are <u>not new suits</u>, and
  therefore are <u>non-forcing</u> bids. These bids are <u>limited</u> bids, as they have an upper
  limit of points, and are called "range" bids.
  Example: Simple raise (6-10) or 1NT (6-10) points.

- Responder <u>limits</u> his hand and his upper point count by the following bids.
  1. The simple raise (6-10) points shows no more than 10 points.
  2. The limit raise of (10-12) points shows no more than 12 points,
  3. 1NT bid (6-10) points shows no more than 10 points.

- Opener's bids are generally non-forcing, and responder can pass.

RESPONDER'S OPTIONS *WITH* SUPPORT FOR PARTNER'S OPENING MAJOR.

Spades used as sample major suit.

Option #1: (6-10) points: The Simple Raise:

Three+cards in partner's suit. Raise partner's suit at the two-level.
Example: Opener 1♠ - Responder 2♠.

Option #2: (10-12) points: The Limit Raise:

Three+cards in partner's suit. Jump to the three-level.
Example: Opener 1♠ - Responder 3♠.

Notice: The 10 point hand is used both for the simple raise and the limit raise.
Explanation: Responder with 10 points and only three-card support, should bid the
simple raise at the two-level.

Responder with 10 points and four-card support can bid the limit raise, as there is now
a known nine-card fit. Responder with 11-12 points and three or four+card support bids
the jump limit raise, as the 11-12 point hand is close to an opening hand.

Option #3: 13-15 points:

Holding 13-15 points, responder can make a forcing bid of his own suit, then bid game in
partner's suit after hearing partner's non-jump rebid.

Option #4: 16+points:

A non-passed (NPH) hand responder makes a forcing bid to learn more about partner's hand,
and then may explore for game or slam.

RESPONDER'S OPTIONS *WITHOUT* SUPPORT FOR PARTNER'S OPENING MAJOR.

Option #5: 6 to a bad 12 points: Bad 12 is less than 2 ½ quick tricks.

A passed hand (PH) responder can bid a new suit at the one-level with 6-12 points;
1NT with (6-10); or 2NT with (11-12) points.

Responder needs at least 10+points to bid a five+card heart suit over 1♠, and at least
10+points to bid any four+card minor at the two-level.

Responder's jump rebid in his suit shows a six+card suit and 11-12 points - invitational.

Option #6: 6+points:

A <u>NPH</u> responder's one-level bid of a new suit is forcing. Opener must bid again for one more round of bidding.

A <u>NPH</u> responder must have a five+card heart suit and 10+points to bid hearts at the two-level over a 1♠ bid, and 10+points to bid any four+card minor suit at the two-level.

Option #7: <u>11-12 points.</u>   <u>13-15 points.</u>

A NPH responder can bid a new suit at the one-level, <u>forcing</u>, and then jump to show a six+card suit and 11-12 points, invitational.

Responder bids 3NT with 13-15 points and a balanced hand - non-forcing.

Option #8: <u>16+points:</u>

Responder makes a <u>forcing</u> bid to learn more about partner's hand, and may explore for slam after hearing partner's rebid.

RESPONDER'S OPTIONS WHEN PARTNER OPENS A MINOR.

Option #9: 6+points:

Responder should bid his four+card major after partner's one-level minor opening bid, especially with weaker hands.

If responder has four cards in both major suits, responder bids the major suits <u>up-the-line</u>, i.e. the four-card heart suit first.

RESPONDER'S NOTRUMP BIDS: Non-forcing

Option #10:

Responder bids a level of notrump with no <u>four+card major</u>, and no 5+card support for partner's minor. Minor support usually shows at least a five-card suit, as opener may have bid a 3+card suit. Responder may have a balanced or an unbalanced hand and no other bid.

Responder's bids:	
6-10 points	Bid 1NT - non-forcing
11-12 points	Jump to 2NT - invitation to game
13-15 points	Jump to 3NT - bid game

#1 Sample hand:

West (Dealer)   East
♠AK1032   1♠   1NT   ♠Q8
♥QJ4   All Pass   ♥10876
♦Q65   ♦K32
♣103   ♣K854

- West with <u>13 points</u> and a five-card spade suit opens the bidding 1♠.
- East with 8 points and <u>two spades</u>, can't make a simple raise of the spade suit.
- East does not have <u>10+points</u> to bid a new suit at the two-level.
- East <u>must</u> bid with 6+points, and bids 1NT (6-10 points.
- West knows there is no spade fit and partner has no more than 10 points.
- The combined partnership points are only 13+10 points = 23 points.
- West passes without the 25-26 points needed for a 3NT game contract.

#2 Sample hand:

West (Dealer)   East
1♥   3♥ (limit raise)
4♥   All Pass

                          North
                          ♠953
                          ♥J98
                          ♦<u>10986</u>
                          ♣A93

West (Dealer)   East
♠108   ♠Q742
♥AQ1054   ♥K763
♦AQJ   ♦K72
♣J86   ♣K10

                          South
                          ♠AK106
                          ♥2
                          ♦543
                          ♣Q7542

- West bids 1♥ with 15 points and a five-card heart suit. East with four hearts upgrades his hand to 12 points, adding one more point for the doubleton club hearing the heart fit. East jumps to 3♥, limit raise (10-12 points).
- Hearing the limit raise showing heart support, West upgrades his hand one point for the doubleton spade. West now has 16 points. West adds East's promise of a minimum 10 point limit raise to his 16 points. 16+10 = 26 points - a major suit game.
- West bids 4♥. North leads the ♦10, top of nothing.

THE FINESSE: More about the finesse in Chapter 6.

The "Finesse" is a form of declarer play of taking tricks by capturing an opponent's honor between declarer's lower and higher honors.

- The finesse allows you to make extra tricks by capturing opponent's honors.

- When you finesse, you play one defender for a certain card holding

- A good way to know if you should finesse is to ask yourself how it would help you if your opponent covers your honor with their honor.

- The finesse gives you a 50/50% chance of capturing an opponent's honors. In general, lead <u>towards</u> the card you hope to take the trick.

Examples:	#1. Dummy	#2. Dummy	#3. Dummy
	QJ6-lead Q	**J83- lead J**	105<u>3</u> - lead 3
	Declarer	Declarer	Declarer
	A108<u>7</u>	AQ10<u>7</u>	<u>K</u>82

- **#1 Play the queen from dummy**. If RHO COVERS your queen with his king, **covering an honor with an honor**, you will play the ace of the suit and capture RHO's king. The finesse is successful

- **#2 Play the jack from dummy**. RHO may <u>not</u> have the king and not cover the jack, and you will allow the jack to **"ride"** into your LHO's hand by playing a low card from your hand and <u>not</u> playing the ace. If LHO has the king, **you have lost the finesse.** However, although you've lost the trick, you have set up three tricks now with the AQ10.

Play a low card up to your honor:

- #3 You are playing RHO for the ace in the suit. **Play a low card from dummy toward the king, the card you want to win the trick**. If RHO plays the ace, your king will be good for a trick. If RHO plays low, you will insert your king.

- If you simply lead out the king, there is a 100% chance an opponent will capture your king with his ace.

- **However, if you lead a low card toward your king, and your RHO has the ace, your king will be good for a trick whether RHO plays the ace or not.** You have finessed against your RHO's ace to win your king. You do not avoid losing a trick to the ace but you do build a winner.

#1

North
♠ J43
♥ A963
♦ 83
♣ Q763

West (Dealer)   East
♠ 10952   ♠ AKQ8
♥ KQ5   ♥ 42
♦ AQ95   ♦ J74
♣ K8   ♣ AJ109

South
♠ 76
♥ J1087
♦ K1062
♣ 542

West is the dealer with _____points and bids_____; North passes; East with_____ points bids_____; South passes; West now with _____points bids_____; North passes; East bids_____; All Pass. What is the contract_____? Who is the declarer_____? Who leads the first card_____? What is the lead___?

#2

North
♠ J3
♥ J98
♦ 109863
♣ A93

West (Dealer)   East
♠ 98   ♠ Q742
♥ AQ1054   ♥ K763
♦ AQ   ♦ K72
♣ Q865   ♣ K7

South
♠ AK1065
♥ 2
♦ J54
♣ J1042

West is the dealer with _____points and bids_____; North passes; East with _____points bids_____; South passes; West bids_____; All Pass. What is the contract_____? Who is the declarer_____? Who leads the first card_____? What is the lead___?

#3   North
                                          ♠92
                                          ♥J762
                                          ♦1082
                                          ♣AK72

West   East
♠AJ764   ♠1053
♥104   ♥Q9
♦KQ7   ♦J963
♣Q103   ♣9854

                                          South (Dealer)
                                          ♠KQ8
                                          ♥AK853
                                          ♦A54
                                          ♣96

South is the dealer with____points and bids ____; West with ____points and bids____;
North with____points bids____; East passes; South now with____points bids____;
West passes; North bids____. Who is the declarer____? Who leads the first card____?
What is the lead___?

#4   North (Dealer)
                                          ♠KQ942
                                          ♥A107
                                          ♦A63
                                          ♣52

West   East
♠1073   ♠AJ
♥92   ♥653
♦10974   ♦Q85
♣K1094   ♣QJ763

                                          South
                                          ♠865
                                          ♥KQJ84
                                          ♦KJ2
                                          ♣A8

North is the dealer with ____points and bids____; East passes; South with ____points
bids____; West passes; North bids____; East passes; South bids____; All Pass.
What is the contract____? Who is the declarer____? Who leads the first card____?
What is the lead___?

#5

North
♠A42
♥AJ6
♦763
♣10543

West
♠10965
♥543
♦AK2
♣AK6

East
♠Q873
♥K98
♦QJ109
♣J8

South (Dealer)
♠KJ
♥Q1072
♦854
♣Q972

South is the dealer and passes; West with___ points bids____; North passes; East with ____points bids____; South passes; West bids____; All Pass. What is the contract____?
Who is the declarer____? Who leads the first card____? What is the lead___?

#6

North
♠J63
♥Q62
♦K10
♣AQ982

West
♠KQ107
♥743
♦J853
♣104

East
♠A8542
♥J9
♦A742
♣J5

South (Dealer)
♠9
♥AK1085
♦Q96
♣K763

South is the dealer with ____points and bids____; West passes; North with ____points bids____; East passes; South bids_____; West passes; North bids___; All Pass.
What is the contract____? Who is the declarer____? Who leads the first card____?
What is the lead___?

#7

North
♠87543
♥A5
♦1072
♣542

West (Dealer)
♠K2
♥KQ10962
♦AQ10
♣103

East
♠QJ9
♥J743
♦J43
♣KQJ

South
♠A106
♥8
♦K965
♣A9876

West is the dealer with _____points and bids_____; East with _____points bids_____; South passes;
West now with _____points bids_____; All Pass.
What is the contract_____? Who is the declarer_____? Who leads the first card_____?
What is the lead____?

#8

North
♠1095
♥K98532
♦108
♣K2

West
♠A64
♥A7
♦J973
♣Q654

East
♠Q832
♥J6
♦KQ62
♣J103

South (Dealer)
♠KJ7
♥Q104
♦A54
♣A987

South is the dealer with _____points and bids_____; West passes; North with _____points
 bids_____; East passes; South with _____points bids_____; West passes; North bids_____;
All Pass. What is the contract_____? Who is the declarer_____? Who leads the first card_____?
What is the lead____?

♟ Answers to practice hands on pages 48-51.

#1

West is the dealer with 14 points and bids 1♦ (no five-card major); North passes; East with 15 points bids 1♠; South passes; West bids 2♠; North passes; East bids 4♠. All Pass.

What is the contract? 4♠. Who is the declarer? East. Who leads the first card? South. What is the lead? ♥J - top of sequence lead.

- **East knows partner has at least a good 12 points to open the bidding.**

- **Hearing support for spades, East upgrades his hand to 16 points by adding one extra point for the doubleton heart.**

- **East's 16 points added to partner's minimum of 12 points equal 28 points.**

- **East bids 4♠, as the partnership has more than the 25-26 needed points for game.**

- **In the play of the hand, East leads the ♦J to finesse South for the ♦K. South covers the ♦J with his ♦K to promote his ♦10.**

#2

West as dealer with 15 points and bids 1♥; North passes; East with 11 points jumps to 3♥ (limit raise); South passes; West bids 4♥; All Pass.

What is the contract? 4♥. Who is the declarer? West. Who leads the first card? North. What is the lead? ♦10.

- **North leads the ♦10, top of a sequence. West upgrades his hand to 16 points with the doubleton spade after hearing heart support from partner.**

- **West's 16 points with partner's minimum 10 point limit raise, equals at least 26 points, and West bids 4♥ game.**

- **The trump suit may not be evenly distributed as in this hand with a 3-1 split in the suit.**

- **West must not first draw trumps. West has two possible losing clubs in his hand. He must first lead a club to the ♣K in dummy to knock out the ♣A. Then, plays the ♣Q, voiding the suit in dummy.**

- **Declarer can trump two losing clubs in the dummy, and will use diamond suit as a "transportation suit" to return to his hand to lead the losing clubs.**

#3

South is the dealer with 17 points and bids 1♥; West with 13 points overcalls 1♠;
North with 9 points bids 2♥, one more point for the doubleton spade with the heart fit.
East passes; South now has 18 points, upgrading his hand one point for the doubleton club with heart support. **South invites North to bid game if he 8-10 points, the upper range of the simple raise. North with 9 points bid 4♥.**

What is the contract? 4♥. Who is the declarer? South. Who leads the first card? West.
What is the lead? ♦K.

- **West leads ♦K top of a sequence. West does not want to lead the unsupported ♠A.**
- **Holding nine trumps, South plays the ♥AK hoping the ♥Q will fall.**

#4

North is the dealer with 14 points and bids 1♠; South now with 16 points (one extra point for the doubleton club with the spade fit) makes a 2♥ forcing bid. South must have 5+hearts and 10+points to bid 2♥ over a 1♠ opening bid. North bids 3♥; South bids 4♥.

What is the contract? 4♥. Who is the declarer? South. Who leads the first card? West.
What is the lead? ♣4 - low from the ♣K honor.

- **South is a non-passed hand, and although holding three spades in support of partner's spade suit, South with 16 points and five hearts bids 2♥ a new suit, forcing bid to learn more about partner's hand.**
- **The heart suit may be a better trump suit than the spade suit.**
- **North knows South must have five hearts and 10+points to bid 2♥ over a 1♠ bid, and bids 3♥ limiting his hand to less than 16 points by not bidding game. South with opening points bid the 4♥ game.**
- **South's 16 points plus North's 12+points = at least 28 points for game.**

#5

South is the dealer and passes; West with 14 points bids 1♣; East with 9 points bids 1♠;
West bids 2♠; All Pass.

What is the contract? 2♠. Who is the declarer? East.
Who leads the first card? South What is the lead? ♦8 - top of nothing lead.

- **West opens 1♣ holding an even number of three cards in both the minor suits.**
- **After hearing West's minimum raise to 2♠, East passes.**
- **A heart must be led from dummy towards East ♥K, finessing North for the ♥A.**

#6

South is the dealer with 13 points and bids 1♥; West passes; North with 14 points, one point for the doubleton diamond with the heart fit. North makes a forcing bid of 2♣ to learn more about partner's hand; East passes; South bids 3♣ (minimum hand); West passes; North bids 4♥; All Pass. What is the contract? 4♥. Who is the declarer? South. Who leads the first card? West. What is the lead? ♠K - top of a sequence.

- **North bids 2♣, a new and a forcing bid, to learn more about South's hand before supporting the heart suit. North knows his opening hand facing partner's opening hand should produce game.**

- **South makes a minimum raise of North's club suit to 3♣, with no extra values. North bids the 4♥ game.**

- **Declarer draws trumps, then plays on clubs to discard a losing diamond.**

#7

West is the dealer with 16 points and bids 1♥; East with 11 points jumps to 3♥ (limit raise), West now with 18 points, two points for doubleton spade and club suits, bids 4♥; All Pass. What is the contract? 4♥. Who is the declarer? West. Who leads the first card? North. What is the lead? ♠8 - top of nothing lead.

- **East's jump limit raise shows at least 10 points.**

- **West counts 18+10 points = 28 points. West bid the 4♥ game.**

- **West counts four losers, and must finesse South for the ♦K by leading ♦J from the dummy.**

- **South seeing the ♦10 in dummy, does not cover the ♦J as he nor partner have the ♦10 to promote by covering the ♦J with the ♦K.**

#8

South is the dealer with 14 points and bids 1♣; West passes; North with 8 points bids 1♥; East passes; South bids 1NT; West passes; North bids 2♥; All Pass. What is the contract? 2♥. Who is the declarer? North. Who leads the first card? East. What is the lead? ♦K - top of sequence.

- **South must have four hearts to raise North's heart suit to the two-level. North is a non-passed hand and made a forcing bid of a new suit. South must bid again, and bids 1NT with a balanced hand.**

- **North rebids his 6-card heart suit preferring to play in a suit contract with his unbalanced hand. South passes as North has made a minimum rebid of hearts.**

 **CHAPTER FOUR**

FRAMEWORK OF BIDDING - PART THREE

JUMPS AND JUMP SHIFTS   *REBIDS BY OPENER AND RESPONDER*

Opener jumps in his suit: 16-18 points unsupported six+card suit...invitational.

Example: Opener bids 1♥... Responder bids either 1♠, 1NT or two of a minor...
Opener jumps to 3♥ with 16-18 points holding such as: ♠x ♥AKQxxx, ♦KQx, ♣Qxx.

Responder jumps in his suit: 11-12 points and an unsupported six+card suit...invitational.

Example: Opener bids 1♣... Responder bids 1♥... Then after opener makes a simple rebid,
responder jumps to 3♥ with 11-12 points holding such as: ♠xx, ♥AKJxxx, ♦Kxx, ♣xx

---

Opener with support of responder's suit: 19-21 points, jumps to game.

Example: Opener 1♦... Responder bids 1♥...
Opener bids 4♥ holding such as: ♠Axxx, ♥AKQx, ♦KQx, ♣xx (one point - doubleton club).

Partner promised 6+points and four+cards in the suit with his one-level response.
Opener counts 19+6 = 25 points needed for game, and bids 4♥.

In this sequence, hearing a game bid from opener showing 19-21 points, responder may then
explore slam possibilities if holding 12+points.

Rebids: A rebid of an unsupported suit promises a six+card suit.

- Try not to rebid an unsupported suit as that call shows a six+card suit.
- However, with 16-18 points, you <u>may rebid a supported five-card major</u>
  <u>as an "invitational bid"</u>. After partner's simple raise (6-10 points) of your
  major, a three-level invitational bid by opener asks partner to bid game if partner is
  at "the top" of his simple raise with 8-10 points, or pass with a bottom range of 6-7 points.

Invitational Bids: Opener or responder can make an invitational bid, inviting partner to
bid game if the combined partnership points add up to game. Partner will pass without the
necessary points for game.

Example: Opener (16-18 points)	1♠	2♠	Responder: (6-10 points)
Opener's rebid <u>invites</u> partner to game.	3♠	?	Responder bids game with 8-10 points or passes with 6-7 points.

#1 Sample jump hand by opener: 16-18 points.
North and South pass throughout the bidding.

Contract: 4♥
Bidding:

West (Dealer)	1♥	1NT	East
♠AK	3♥	4♥	♠109
♥AK9875			♥Q6
♦Q97			♦J1062
♣95			♣AJ432

- West with 18 points bids 1♥.
- East bids 1NT with 9 points. East does not have three+card heart suit to support partner's hearts, or 10 points to bid 2♣, a new suit at the two-level.
- West JUMPS to 3♥ showing 16-18 points and six+card heart suit.
- With two hearts, East knows there is an eight+card heart fit, and upgrades his hand one point for the doubleton spade. West has shown 16-18 points.
- 16+10 = 26 game points. East bids 4♥.

#2 Sample jump hand by responder: 11-12 points.
North and South pass throughout the bidding.

Contract: 4♥
Bidding:

West (Dealer)				East
♠KQ7	1♦	1♥		♠82
♥1043	1NT	3♥		♥KQ9876
♦AKQ6	4♥			♦94
♣1084				♣AJ9

- West with 14 points and no five-card major bids 1♦.
- East with 12 points bids 1♥, a new suit and a forcing bid by a non-passed hand.
- East is promising partner at least a four-card heart suit and 6+points at this point in the bidding. West has only three hearts, and needs at least a four-card heart suit to support partner's suit
- West bids 1NT, showing a minimum balanced hand, no convenient suit to bid.
- East jumps to 3♥, showing a six+card heart suit (a rebid of an <u>unsupported suit</u> shows a six+card suit), and an invitational hand of 11-12 points.
- Now West's three hearts creates a nine-card ideal fit.
- West's 14 points and East's minimum 11 points = 25 points for game.
- West bids 4♥.

#3 Sample jump hand by opener:

Contract: 4♥   West leads ♠K
Bidding:

South (Dealer)	West	North	East
1♥	Pass	2♥	Pass
4♥	All Pass		

North
♠632
♥Q642
♦K102
♣K42

West
♠KQ107
♥73
♦J9835
♣Q10

East
♠AJ54
♥J9
♦74
♣98653

South (Dealer)
♠98
♥AK1085
♦AQ6
♣AJ7

- South opens 1♥ with 19 points and a five-card heart suit, 18 HCP, adding and one extra point for the fifth heart to equal 19 points.

- North has 8 points and a four-card heart suit for his simple raise of 6-10 points promising at least three hearts to create the eight-card fit.

- Now that South knows there is a fit in the hearts with partner, South can re-evaluate his hand, adding one more point for his doubleton ♠98.

- South now has 20 points and counts at least 6 points responder promised with his simple raise to 2♥ showing (6-10 points). South has at least 26 points needed for game and bids 4♥.

- West leads the ♠K, top of a sequence.

- South counts two spade losers and one club loser. South has a contract of 4♥ and can lose three tricks. There are a total of thirteen available tricks, and South needs 10 tricks to make his contract. South makes the 4♥ contract.

JUMP SHIFTS: A jump shift is a jump into a <u>new suit</u> by either player.

Opener jump shifts into a new suit to show 19-21 points.

- The jump shift by opener in a suit contract creates a *game-forcing* auction.
- Opener can also jump shift into 2NT with 18-19 points and a balanced hand. The jump shift into 2NT is NOT a game-forcing auction. Responder can pass with a weak hand.

Responder makes a forcing bid with 16+points.

- Responder makes a forcing bid to learn more about partner's hand, and then may jump shift to explore for slam.

Sample jump shift hand by opener: 19 - 21 points
East and West pass throughout the bidding.

Contract 4♥
North (Dealer)

North	1♠	1NT	South
♠AK652	<u>3♥</u>	4♥	♠108
♥AKQ2			♥109864
♦Q109			♦K10
♣7			♣KJ109

- North with 19 points opens the bidding 1♠.

- South can't bid 2♠ holding only two cards in the suit, or 2♣ without 10+points to bid a new suit at the two-level.

- South with 8 points (one point for the fifth heart) bids 1NT.

- North <u>JUMP SHIFTS</u> TO 3♥, game forcing.

- South has a five-card heart suit, and opener promises at least 3 or more hearts. Usually a jump shift will show 4+cards in the suit. A 3-card suit may be bid if necessary to show the jump shift.

- South now has 10 points (one point each for spade and diamond doubletons with a heart fit). South bids the 4♥ game, knowing the partnership has at least 19 + 10 points = 29 points and a heart fit.

AT A GLANCE (spades sample suit)

#1 Responder _with_ support for partner.

	Opener	Responder
6-10 points - low	1♠	2♠ Simple raise
10-12 points - medium	1♠	3♠ Limit raise (usually 4 trumps)

13-15 points - high		Bid a _forcing_ new suit at the one or two-level, and rebid game in partner's suit, after a non-jump bid by partner.
16+points - highest - bid new suit		With 17+points, responder makes a forcing bid to learn more about partner's hand, then may jump shift explore for slam.

#2 Opener's rebid after hearing support from partner.

	Opener	Responder	Rebids by Opener
12-15 points - low	1♠	2♠	Pass
16-18 points - medium	1♠	2♠	3♠ Invite game
19-20 points - high	1♠	2♠	4♠ Bid game

#3 Opener's rebid in support of responder's suit.

	Opener	Responder	Rebids by Opener
12-15 points - low	1♥	1♠	2♠ Raise to the two-level
16-18 points - medium	1♥	1♠	3♠ Three-level, invite game
19-20 points - high	1♥	1♠	4♠ Four level, bid game

CAPTAIN OF THE HAND: Either the opener or responder can become the "captain" of the hand. Being the captain means you are the player who will take charge of the bidding after partner limits his hand.

Example: Opener bids 1♠ Responder bids 2♠ (6-10) points. Responder's 2♠ bid has limited his hand to a maximum of 10 points. Opener as captain, can pass, invite or bid game. However, when opener invites responder to game, responder now becomes the captain as to whether to pass or accept opener's invitation and bid game.

There are sayings in Bridge such as "The one who knows goes" (to game), and the one who doesn't know "invites" (partner to game). The Framework of Bidding Bridge language is a mathematical guideline to enable your partnership to bid accurately. It's important to remember and play by the rules. However, as you continue to play Bridge, you'll bring an understanding of when you can modify the rules for certain types of hands. You'll apply creative thinking in your bidding decisions, and the challenge of applying the elements of your hand within the Framework of Bidding process is why Bridge remains an exciting and evolving game.

Practice hands: Answers on pages 64-65.

#1 North (Dealer)
♠AK2
♥AKQ987
♦97
♣98

West   East
♠J643   ♠Q75
♥542   ♥J10
♦K854   ♦AJ32
♣J5   ♣K764

                          South
                          ♠1098
                          ♥63
                          ♦Q106
                          ♣AQ1032

North is the dealer with _____points and bids_____; East passes; South with ___points
bids_____; West passes; North bids____; East passes; South bids____; All Pass.
What is the contract_____? Who is the declarer_____? Who leads the first card____?
What is the lead___?

#2 North (Dealer)
♠AK652
♥AKQ2
♦Q109
♣2

West   East
♠Q94   ♠J73
♥753   ♥J4
♦A632   ♦754
♣KQ9   ♣J10853

                          South
                          ♠108
                          ♥10986
                          ♦KJ8
                          ♣A764

North is the dealer with _____points and bids_____; East passes; South with ___points
bids_____; West passes; North bids____; East passes; South bids____; All Pass. What is the
contract_____? Who is the declarer_____? Who leads the first card____? What is the lead___?

#3

North
♠J953
♥A86
♦95
♣J543

West (Dealer)
♠4
♥Q73
♦AKQ108
♣AK109

East
♠AK7
♥J542
♦632
♣Q76

South
♠Q10862
♥K109
♦J74
♣82

West is the dealer with _____points and bids_____; North passes; East with ____points
bids_____; South passes; West bids____; North passes; East bids____; All Pass.
What is the contract_____? Who is the declarer_____? Who leads the first card_____?
What is the lead____?

#4

North
♠J93
♥862
♦A52
♣J1065

West (Dealer)
♠10862
♥AKQ73
♦84
♣AQ

East
♠AK74
♥J5
♦J973
♣432

South
♠Q5
♥1094
♦K1096
♣K987

West is the dealer with _____points and bids____; North passes; East with_____ points
bids_____; South passes; West now with _____point bids____; North passes; East bids____; All
Pass. What is the contract____? Who is the declarer____? Who leads the first card_____?
What is the lead____?

#5

North (Dealer)
♠KQ1064
♥AK1062
♦95
♣9

West
♠A75
♥Q7
♦K4
♣1086532

East
♠J
♥J543
♦QJ632
♣KQ4

South
♠9832
♥98
♦A1087
♣AJ7

North is the dealer with _____points and bids_____; East passes; South with ___points bids_____; West passes; North bids_____; All Pass. What is the contract____? Who is the declarer____? Who leads the first card____? What is the lead___?

#6

North
♠QJ1073
♥83
♦Q2
♣KQ86

West
♠A4
♥9542
♦AJ1076
♣32

East
♠92
♥K6
♦K9853
♣J1075

South (Dealer)
♠K865
♥AQJ107
♦4
♣A94

South is the dealer with _____points and bids ___; West passes; North with _____points bids_____; East passes; South now with____ points bids ___; West passes; North bids_____; All Pass. What is the contract____? Who is the declarer____? Who leads the first card____? What is the lead___?

62

#7

North
♠42
♥A10876
♦KJ8
♣A43

West
♠96
♥K54
♦9432
♣K875

East
♠Q87
♥QJ32
♦A107
♣Q62

South (Dealer)
♠AKJ1053
♥9
♦Q65
♣J109

South is the dealer with _____points and bids_____; West passes; North with _____points bids_____; East passes; South bids_____: West passes; North bids____; All Pass.
What is the contract_____? Who is the declarer_____? Who leads the first card_____?
What is the lead____?

#8

North (Dealer)
♠98
♥Q76
♦J108
♣A8753

West
♠10654
♥K942
♦Q54
♣J6

East
♠AKQJ32
♥A103
♦32
♣K10

South
♠7
♥J85
♦AK976
♣Q942

North is the dealer and passes; East with ____points bids_____; South bids____; West with _____points bids_____; North passes; East bids_____; All Pass. What is the contract_____?
Who is the declarer_____? Who leads the first card_____? What is the lead____?

Answers practice hands on page 60 - 63.

#1

North is the dealer with 18 points and bids 1♥; East passes; South with 9 points bids 1NT;
West passes; North jumps to 3♥; East passes; South bids 4♥; All Pass.
What is the contract? 4♥. Who is the declarer? North. Who leads the first card? East.
What is the lead? ♥J. North shows 16-18 points and a six-hearts by his jump to 3♥.

- **East does not want to lead away from honors in the club and diamond suits, and leads the ♥J.**
- **North counts four losers and must finesse by leading a low club from his hand toward dummy's ♣AQ, playing the ♣Q, playing East for the ♣K.**

#2

North is the dealer with 19 points and bids 1♠; East passes; South with 8 points and only two
spades bids 1NT; West passes; North bids 3♥ (jump shift); East passes; South bids 4♥; All Pass.
What is the contract? 4♥. Who is the declarer? North. Who leads the first card? East.
What is the lead? ♣J - top of sequence lead.

- **North's jump shift in hearts shows 19-21 points. South with four hearts bids 4♥.**
- **North draws only two rounds of trump, plays the ♠AK, and must ruff a spade loser before pulling the last trump.**

#3

West is the dealer with 19 points and bids 1♦; North passes; East with 10 points bids 1♥;
South passes; West bids 3♣ (jump shift); North passes; East bids 3NT; All Pass.
What is the contract? 3NT. Who is the declarer? East. Who leads the first card? South.
What is the lead? ♠6 - fourth card down in his longest and strongest suit (more in chapter 5).

- **After West's jump shift with 19-21 points; East with a balanced hand, bids 3NT game. South will try to set up his spade suit by leading the ♠6, the fourth card down from his longest and strongest suit (more in Chapter six).**

#4

West is the dealer with 16 points and bids 1♥; North passes; East with 9 points bids 1♠;
South passes; West jumps to 3♠ with 18 points, one point each for doubleton diamond and club
suits with a spade fit; North passes; East bids 4♠; All Pass. What is the contract? 4♠. Who is the
declarer? East. Who leads the first card? South. What is the lead? ♦6 – low from an honor.

- **East counts four possible losers. One spade, one club and two diamonds.**
- **East must finesse by leading a low club from his hand toward dummy's ♣AQ, playing the ♣Q in dummy and hoping South holds the ♣K. The finesse wins.**

#5

North is the dealer with 14 points and bids 1♠; South with 10 points bids a limit raise of 3♠, adding one point for the doubleton heart. North bids 4♠ now with 17 points with the spade fit, adding two points for the singleton club, and one point for the doubleton diamond. All Pass. What is the contract? 4♠.Who is the declarer? North. Who leads the first card? East. What is the lead? ♣K - top of a sequence.

- **North, holding 5-5 cards in two suits bid the suits down the line, the higher ranking suit first. North plays ♣A, and then a low spade toward his ♠K. West plays a low spade. North must play the ♥AK, and trump two losing hearts in dummy by playing the highest trump in dummy to "set up" the heart suit before pulling opponent's remaining trumps. West can decide to play the ♠A to overruff the ♠9 in dummy.**

#6

South is the dealer with 15 points and bids 1♥; North with 11 points bids 1♠; South jumps to 3♠ with 17 points, adding two points for the singleton diamond with the spade fit. North bids 4♠; All Pass. What is the contract? 4♠.Who is the declarer? North. Who leads the first card? East. What is the lead? ♣J - top of a sequence.

- **North counts four losers, and must trump one diamond in dummy. After drawing opponent's trumps, North plays a low heart toward dummy's ♥AQ in dummy, playing the ♥Q to finesse East's ♥K. The finesse is successful.**

#7

South is the dealer with 13 points and bids 1♠; West passes; North with 13 points bids 2♥; East passes; South bids 2♠; West passes; North bids 4♠; All Pass.
What is the contract? 4♠; Who is the declarer? South; Who leads the first card? West;
What is the lead? 5♣ - low from the ♣K honor.

- **South's rebids the spade suit promising a six-card suit. North with an opening hand and two spades, knows there is an eight-card spade fit, game values and bids 4♠. South counts four loses and must finesse East for the ♠Q.**

#8

North is the dealer and passes; East with 19 points bids 1♠; South bids 2♦; West bids 2♠, adding one point for the doubleton club with a spade fit. East now with 22 points bids 4♠, adding two points for the singleton diamond. All Pass. What is the contract? 4♠. Who is the declarer? East. Who leads the first card? South. What is the lead? ♦A - A from AK.

- **Declarer bids 4♠ with at least 28 combined points. Declarer counts 5 possible losers. After drawing trumps, Declarer plays a heart to dummy's ♥K and a club toward his ♣K; North plays the ♣A and leads a diamond to South ♦AK. Declare can now sluff a losing heart on dummy's ♦Q. The defense takes two diamonds and a club, and East makes the 4♠ contract.**

#1

North
♠J7
♥Q1082
♦8652
♣A105

West   East (Dealer)
♠Q109   ♠AK6532
♥954   ♥AK
♦A1093   ♦74
♣QJ3   ♣942

South
♠84
♥J763
♦KQJ
♣K876

East is the dealer with _____points and bids_____; South passes; West with _____points bids_____; North passes; East bids _____; South passes; West bids_____; All Pass. What is the contract_____? Who is the declarer_____? Who leads the first card_____? What is the lead___?

#2

North
♠AQ107
♥J8
♦532
♣QJ83

West   East
♠J43   ♠92
♥9432   ♥653
♦A97   ♦KJ1085
♣K62   ♣A1075

South (Dealer)
♠K865
♥AKQ107
♦Q64
♣9

South is dealer with _____points and bids_____; West passes; North with _____points bids___; East passes; South with _____points bids_____; West passes; North bids_____; All Pass. What is the contract_____? Who is the declarer_____? Who leads the first card_____? What is the lead___?

#3

North
♠Q102
♥KJ8
♦Q942
♣A108

West
♠643
♥Q1093
♦A65
♣642

East
♠J98
♥A652
♦K73
♣753

South (Dealer)
♠AK75
♥74
♦J108
♣KQJ9

South is the dealer with _____points and bids ____; West passes; North with ____points bids____; East passes; South bids ____; All Pass. What is the contract____? Who is the declarer____? Who leads the first card____? What is the lead___?

#4

North
♠8632
♥82
♦9742
♣K86

West
♠Q104
♥Q973
♦AJ5
♣J104

East (Dealer)
♠J9
♥AKJ106
♦K1063
♣A7

South
♠AK75
♥54
♦Q8
♣Q9532

East is the dealer with _____points and bids ____; South passes; West with ____points bids____; North passes; East bids____; All Pass. What is the contract____? Who is the declarer____? Who leads the first card____? What is the lead___?

#5

North (Dealer)
♠KQ54
♥A108
♦AQ742
♣6

West
♠A86
♥9732
♦1086
♣KQ8

East
♠10
♥J654
♦J3
♣AJ10752

South
♠J9732
♥KQ
♦K95
♣943

North is the dealer with _____points and bids ____; East passes; South with ____points bids____; West passes; North with ___points bids____; East passes; South bids____; All Pass. What is the contract____? Who is the declarer____? Who leads the first card____? What is the lead___?

#6

North (Dealer)
♠Q1063
♥J83
♦KQ6
♣1082

West
♠74
♥AQ95
♦J10943
♣96

East
♠5
♥K10762
♦752
♣AJ53

South
♠AKJ982
♥4
♦A8
♣KQ74

North is the dealer and passes; East passes; South with ____points bids_____; West passes; North bids____; East passes; South bids____; All Pass. What is the contract____? Who is the declarer____? Who leads the first card____? What is the lead___?

#7

North
♠QJ1073
♥83
♦52
♣KQ82

West
♠A4
♥9542
♦KJ1076
♣63

East
♠92
♥K6
♦AQ98
♣J10754

South (Dealer)
♠K865
♥AQJ107
♦43
♣A9

South is the dealer with _____points and bids _____; West passes; North with _____points bids_____; East passes; South bids_____; West passes; North bids_____; All Pass. What is the contract_____? Who is the declarer_____? Who leads the first card_____? What is the lead___?

#8

North (Dealer)
♠42
♥876
♦AKJ1098
♣A3

West
♠9653
♥1092
♦6
♣KJ875

East
♠107
♥AKQJ4
♦42
♣10964

South
♠AKQJ8
♥53
♦Q753
♣Q2

North is the dealer with _____points and bids _____; East overcalls_____; South bids_____; West passes; North bids_____; East passes; South bids_____; All Pass.
What is the contract_____? Who is the declarer_____? Who leads the first card_____?
What is the lead___?

69

👫 Answers to practice hands on pages 66 - 69.

#1

East is the dealer with 16 points and bids 1♠; South passes; West with 9 points bids 2♠;
North passes; East now with 18 points adding two points for the doubleton diamond and heart suits
with the spade fit and bids 3♠, invitational. South passes; West bids 4♠. All Pass.
What is the contract? 4♠. Who is the declarer? East. Who leads the first card? South.
What is the lead? ♦K - top of sequence lead.

- **East is not sure of partnership game points and makes an invitational bid
  of 3♠ to invite partner to bid game if he has 8-9-10 of his simple raise.**
- **West with 9 points accepts the invitation, and bids the 4♠ game.**
- **After drawing trumps, declarer leads up to the ♣QJ twice to score his tenth trick**

#2

South is the dealer with 15 points and bids 1♥; West passes; North with 9 points bids 1♠;
East passes; South now with 17 points jumps to 3♠, adding two points for the singleton club with a
spade fit, and West passes; North bids 4♠; All Pass. What is the contract? 4♠. Who is the declarer?
North. Who leads the first card? East. What is the lead? ♦J – top of the interior sequence.

- **Defenders win three diamond tricks by trapping dummy's ♦Q with the lead of the
  ♦J. East plays the ♣A with the singleton club in dummy. Defenders win four tricks
  defeating the 4♠ contract. It happens with good defense!**

#3

South is the dealer with 14 points and bids 1♣; West passes; North with 12 points jumps
to 2NT with 11-12 points, no four-card major. East passes; South bids 3NT; All Pass.
What is the contract? 3NT. Who is the declarer? North. Who leads the first card? East.
What is the lead? ♥2 – fourth card down in his longest suit.

- **North counts seven winners in the spade and club suits, and needs two more tricks
  to make the 3NT contract. Declarer hopes the spade suit provides one more
  trick if the suit breaks 3-3. Declarer plans to play the spade suit first. Declarer wins
  the heart lead in his hand with the ♥K. West playing ♥Q. North plays the spade suit
  followed by the club suit. The 3NT contracts makes as spades provides the extra
  trick with the ♠5 in dummy. One heart, four spades and four clubs = 9 tricks**

#4

East is the dealer with 17 points and bids 1♥; South passes; West with 10 points
and four hearts jumps to 3♥ (limit raise); North passes: East bids 4♥; All Pass.
What is the contract? 4♥. Who is the declarer? East. Who leads the first card? South.
What is the lead? ♠A - ace from AK

- **Declarer counts four possible losers and plans to eliminate one diamond
  loser by finessing South for the ♦Q.**

#5

North is the dealer with 16 points and bids 1♦; East passes; South with 10 points bids 1♠; West passes; North now with 18 points (two points for the singleton club with a spade fit) jumps to 3♠; East passes; South bids 4♠; All Pass.
What is the contract? 4♠. Who is the declarer? South. Who leads the first card? West. What is the lead? ♣K - top of a sequence.

- **North's jump to 3♠ shows 16-18 points - invitational.**

#6

North is the dealer and passes; East passes; South with 19 points bids 1♠; West passes; North bids 2♠; East passes; South now with 22 points (two points for the singleton heart and one point for the doubleton diamond with a spade fit) bids 4♠; All Pass.
What is the contract? 4♠. Who is the declarer? South. Who leads the first card? West. What is the lead? ♦J - top of a sequence.

- **Declarer counts two losers, one in each of the heart and club suit, making an overtrick in the 4♠ contract.**

#7

South is the dealer with 15 points and bids 1♥; West passes; North with 9 points bids 1♠; East passes; South now with 17 points (two points for the club and diamond doubletons with a fit in the spade suit) jumps to 3♠; North reevaluates his hand to 11 points (two points for the heart and diamond doubletons after partner's support for spades); North bids 4♠; All Pass.
What is the contract? 4♠. Who is the declarer? North. Who leads the first card? East. What is the lead? ♣J - top of a sequence.

- **Declarer counts three losers, one spade and two diamonds, and a possible heart loser.**
- **Declarer must finesse the ♥K by leading a low heart toward dummy's ♥AQ playing East for the ♥K. The finesse is successful and North makes 4♠.**

#8

North is the dealer with 14 points and bids 1♦; East overcalls 1♥; South bids 1♠; West passes; North bids 3♦; East passes; South bids 5♦. All Pass.
What is the contract? 5♦. Who is the declarer? North. Who leads the first card? East. What is the lead? ♥A - A from AK.

- **Declarer counts two heart losers and a club loser.**
- **East plays the ♥AK and switches to the ♣10.**
- **Declarer wins the ♣A, pulls opponents trumps and discards the losing club on the good spade tricks in dummy.**

 **REVIEW OF THE FRAMEWORK OF BIDDING**

OPENER:

1. Open suits at the one-level with a good 12+HCP and + length points.
2. Standard American System requires a five+card major to open a major suit at the one-level. Holding no 5-card major, open a three+card minor.
3. Open 1♦ with four diamonds. Usually open 1♣ with 3-3 in both minors.
4. Do <u>not</u> count short suit points until you find at least an eight+card fit in a suit with partner.
5. Opener's bids and rebids are usually nonforcing calls.
6. Holding two five-card suits, open the higher-ranking suit first, and bid <u>the suits "down" the line</u>.
7. Don't rebid an <u>unsupported</u> five-card suit as a rebid of the suit shows a six+card suit.
8. You can rebid a five-card <u>supported</u> suit as an invitational bid.
9. Jump shifts in a new suit (19-21 points) create game-forcing auctions.
10. Jump shifts to 2NT (18-19 points), are not game forcing.

RESPONDER:

1. Responder must bid with 6+HCP and length points.
2. A new suit by a NPH responder is forcing for opener to bid at least one more time. A PH responder's bids are non-forcing bids.
3. At the one-level, a new suit shows 6+points and four+cards in the suit.
4. At the two-level, a new suit shows 10+points and 5+cards in the heart suit over a 1♠ opener, or four+cards in any minor suit.
5. A NPH responder does not have to jump at his first bid to show a strong hand. Responder makes a forcing bid of a new suit, and later shows strength by his rebid.
6. Responding to opener's minor suit holding 4-4 cards in two major suits, bid the lower-ranking suit first, bidding the suits <u>"up" the line.</u>
7. When partner opens a minor, responder bids a four+card major before supporting opener's minor. Responder should try to bid the four+card major first with a weaker hand.
8. Don't count short suit points until you find an eight+card fit in a suit with partner.
9. Don't rebid an <u>unsupported</u> five-card suit, as a rebid of the suit shows a six+card suit. You can rebid a five-card <u>supported</u> suit as an invitational bid.
10. Jump rebids in your suit show six+cards in the suit and 11-12 points, invitational. Jump raises or preference in partner's suit shows three+support and 11-12 points, invitational.
11. Responder can make a forcing bid with 13-15 points, then jump to game in partner's suit after partner's non-jump rebid.
12. Responder with 16+points makes a forcing bid, and with certain strong hands, may jump shift to explore slam possibilities.

CHAPTER FIVE

NOTRUMP BIDDING   *STAYMAN*   *LEADS IN NOTRUMP*

OPENING 1NT REQUIREMENTS: 15 - 17 High Card Points
No singletons - No voids - Only one doubleton - No short suit points.
Sample Hand: ♠AKJ10, ♥Q85 ♦J83, ♣ A54 = 15 points.

You learned you need nine tricks and at least 25 to 26 combined partnership points to make a 3NT game. Winning tricks can only be made with the highest cards in each suit, as there is no trump suit to win tricks. You win tricks with high cards, and with small cards in long suits after the suit has been played a number of times.

Before playing to the first trick in a notrump contract, declarer should count the winning tricks in the declarer and dummy hands to determine the number of additional tricks needed to make the contract. Winning tricks are running suits such as AKQJ, A, or A and K in the same suit in both the declarer and dummy hands.

Winning Tricks: Declarer: ♠AKJ   ♥J85   ♦A8   ♣A10542   4 winners - ♠AK ♦A ♣A

                Dummy: ♠987   ♥A432   ♦KJ2   ♣KJ   3 winners - ♥A   ♦K   ♣K

There are seven winners in the above example in the declarer and dummy hands. Declarer needs two more tricks to make the 3NT contract, and will play clubs first, as it's declarer's longest suit. The short suits will not provide the needed extra tricks.

The 2♣ Stayman Convention:
A convention is an <u>artificial</u> bid that conveys a different meaning than your actual bid. The 2♣ Stayman convention does not show clubs.

Responder's 2♣ bid asks the 1NT opener to bid his four-card major, and bid them up-the-line if holding both four-card majors.

- Responder must have <u>8+points and at least one four-card major</u>.
- Stayman says nothing about the club suit.
- A responder with less than 8 points must pass and not bid Stayman.

Why use Stayman?
Stayman is used as a tool to have the notrump opener bid a suit first and become the declarer and the concealed hand.

- When the notrump opener is the declarer, the initial lead from LHO of declarer is likely to play "into" declarer's hand, protecting declarer's honors, as declarer is last to play.
- Stayman is used to find a 4-4 fit in a major suit contract. The 1NT opener or responder may have an unguarded doubleton suit, and the major fit may be a better contract than a notrump contract.

Opener <u>with</u> a four-card major: Opener bids the four-card major, or holding both majors, bids the majors "up the line" - the lowest ranking suit first.

Responder: <u>8-9 points</u>: <u>With opener's major</u>, three-level bid <u>inviting</u> game in the major.

<u>10-14 points</u>: With opener's major, bid game in the major.

<u>8-9 points</u>: *Without* opener's major, bid 2NT to <u>invite</u> a 3NT game.

<u>10-14 points</u>: *Without* opener's major, bid 3NT game.

Opener *without* a four-card major: Opener with no four-card major bids 2♦ - artificial. The 2♦ artificial bid denies a major, and the partnership will typically play in a notrump contract.

Responder after opener's 2♦ response:

<u>8-9 points</u>: Bid 2NT to <u>invite</u> game in 3NT.

<u>10-14 points</u>: Bid 3NT or game.

Exception: Responder should probably <u>not</u> use Stayman with 4-3-3-3 or 3-4-3-3 hand. Raise to 2NT with 9 points or bid 3NT with 10-14 points. Although you have a four-card major, your hand is balanced with no ruffing value, and may play better in a notrump contract.

Notrump Bids at a Glance

OPENER	BIDS	POINTS
No voids, no singletons. No more than one doubleton.	1NT	15-17 points
Stayman response with no four-card major. With a four-card major, bid the major in response to Stayman	2♦ response to Stayman 2♥/2♠ with both, bid lower ranking first	
RESPONDER	**BIDS**	
No four-card major.	Pass	0-8 points
With four-card major. Rebid three of the major-invite. Rebid four of the major-game	2♣ Stayman 3-level of opener's major 4-level of opener's major	8+points 9 points 10-14 points
No major fit - invite game	2NT	9 points
No major fit - bid game	3NT	10-14 points

#1 Sample Stayman hand:

Contract: 3NT   East leads ♣6
Bidding:

North (Declarer)	East	South	West
1NT	Pass	2♣ (Stayman)	Pass
2♦ (no 4-card major)	Pass	3NT	All Pass

```
                        North (Dealer)
                        ♠73
                        ♥AQ5
                        ♦K1082
                        ♣AQ43
West                                          East
♠K1098                                        ♠654
♥K86                                          ♥743
♦9763                                         ♦QJ4
♣J5                                           ♣K107**6**
                        South
                        ♠AQJ2
                        ♥J1092
                        ♦A5
                        ♣982
```

Declarer counts five winners (one club, two diamonds, one heart and one spade), and must set up an additional four winners to make the 3NT contract.
Declarer will develop those tricks by finessing for ♥K and ♠K.

- East leads the 6♣ (fourth card from East's longest and strongest suit), next dummy's ♣8, West ♣J, and won by declarer's ♣Q.
- Declarer plays the ♠3 to dummy's ♠J. West plays the ♠K.
  This finesse has lost, however, dummy's ♠AQ are now good tricks.
- West returns a club. North plays the ♣A and plays a low diamond to the ♦A in dummy, and now plays the ♥J from dummy and lets the ♥J "ride", (a finesse term allowing the card into the last to play). The ♥J wins the trick.
- West did not cover the ♥J with his ♥K as he sees the ♥109 in dummy, nothing to promote.
- Dummy continues with the ♥10, West plays a low heart and declarer plays the ♥Q and ♥A dropping the ♥K. The ♥10 is now good in the dummy.
- North plays a spade to the good ♠AJ in dummy.

North has two spade tricks, four heart tricks, two diamond tricks and two club tricks for a total of ten tricks, making his 3NT contract and an overtrick.

#2 Sample Stayman hand:

Contract: 4♠   West leads the ♦Q

Bidding:

South (Dealer)	West	North	East
1NT	Pass	2♣ (Stayman)	Pass
2♠	Pass	4♠	All Pass

North
♠AQ65
♥A832
♦7
♣10964

West
♠94
♥Q54
♦QJ1093
♣QJ8

East
♠J87
♥J109
♦K852
♣752

South (Dealer)
♠K1032
♥K76
♦A64
♣AK3

- South with 17 points opens the bidding 1NT.
- North bids Stayman with ten points and a four-card spade suit, asking South to bid his four-card major.
- South bids 2♠ showing his four-card spade suit, denying a four-card heart suit.
- North bids the game of 4♠. North can reevaluate his hand to 12 points (counting his singleton diamond suit with a fit in the spade suit).
- As South opened 1NT showing 15-17 points, North knows there are at least 27 points in the partnership hands, and at least eight spades for the spade fit.

South counts his losers in the suit contract, a club and heart loser and possibly two diamond losers. Four losers, one too many to make the contract.

South delays pulling opponent's trumps. After winning the ♦A, declarer trumps two diamond losers in the dummy, using club entrys to return to his hand. South plays dummy's ♠AQ, then comes back to the ♥A to draw the last trump with the ♠K, gives up a club setting up the 13th club in dummy. South makes an overtrick in the 4♠ contract.

LEADS IN NOTRUMP CONTRACTS:

There is usually a race between the defenders and the declarer to set up long suits held by each partnership in a notrump contract.

The defender's opening lead is often an attempt to set up a long suit to establish tricks in the suit after knocking out declarer's stoppers in defender's suit. Declarer will also attempt to establish his long suit for the extra tricks needed to make the contract.

Defender's Opening Lead:

- Lead the fourth card down in your longest and strongest suit.
  Example: K108<u>7</u>4.
- You <u>MAY</u> lead away from your four or five-card suit headed by an ace against a notrump contract. Example: Ax<u>x</u>x, or an AQx<u>x</u>.

Why? As there is no trump suit, you are safe to under-lead the ace of a suit

- Promotion: Lead top of a <u>three-card</u> sequence to promote lower honors in the suit. Example: <u>K</u>QJ32. You may also lead the top card from a two-card sequence when you have the card one below your sequence -- such as <u>Q</u>J932 or <u>K</u>Q1032.
- With a two-card sequence, without a nearby touching card, lead fourth card down. Example: KQ8<u>7</u>5
- Lead interior card of a "broken" sequence.
  Example: K<u>J</u>109
- Holding two five-card suits, lead the strongest suit.
- Holding two four-card suits in the major and minor suits, usually lead the major, unless the opponents' bidding has warned you off the major.

What do you Lead in a Notrump Contract?

♠KQJ87_____   ♠QJ932_____
♠KJ108_____   ♣A8653_____
♥QJ8652_____   ♠10987_____
♠AQ875_____   ♠KQ1032_____
♠A432_____   ♦KQ54_____

 Answers to Leads in a Notrump Contract.

♠<u>K</u>QJ87 top of a 3-card sequence   ♠<u>Q</u>J932   top of a broken sequence
♠K<u>J</u>108 top of an interior sequence   ♣A86<u>5</u>3   fourth in longest and strongest suit
♥QJ8<u>6</u>52 fourth in longest and strongest suit   ♠<u>10</u>987   top of a 3-card sequence.
♠AQ8<u>7</u>5 fourth in longest and strongest suit   ♠<u>K</u>Q1032 top of a broken sequence
♠A4<u>3</u>2   fourth in longest and strongest suit   ♦KQ5<u>4</u>   fourth in longest and strongest suit

Open 1NT with <u>15 - 17 High Card Points</u>
No singletons - No voids - Only one doubleton
No short suit points

Declarer should count winning tricks in the declarer and dummy hands to determine the number of additional tricks needed to make the notrump contract. Winning tricks are running suits such as AKQJ, A, or A and K as a combined holding in both the declarer and dummy hands.

Declarer will attempt to set up his longest suit to provide the extra tricks needed to fulfill the contract. Short suits will not provide extra tricks; however can be used as "transportation suits" between the dummy and declarer hands. The defenders will also try to set up their longest suit to defeat the contract.

The 2♣ Stayman bid by responder asks the 1NT opener to bid his four-card major.
- Responder has <u>8+points</u> and <u>one or both four-card majors.</u>

Opener with a major bids a four-card major, or bids majors "up the line" holding both majors.

When opener bids a major:

Responder: <u>8-9 points:</u> <u>WITH opener's major,</u> bid to the three-level
to invite game in the major
<u>10-14 points:</u> <u>WITH opener's major,</u> bid game in the major.
<u>8-9 points:</u> *WITHOUT* opener's major, bids 2NT to invite 3NT.
<u>10-14 points:</u> *WITHOUT* opener's major, bid 3NT game.

Opener bids 2♦ to deny a major: The partnership will play in a 2NT or 3NT.

Responder: <u>8-9 points:</u> Bid 2NT to <u>invite</u> game.
<u>10-14 points:</u> Bid 3NT game.

Leads in notrump contracts:

- You <u>MAY</u> lead away from a <u>long suit headed by an A or AQ</u> in a notrump contract.
- Usually lead the fourth card down in your longest and strongest suit.
- Lead top of a three+card sequence to promote lower honors in the suit. <u>K</u>QJxx
- Lead top card in the interior sequence (K<u>J</u>1076), or top of a broken sequence (<u>Q</u>J932).
- Holding two five card suits, lead the fourth card down in the strongest suit.
- Holding two equivalent four-card major and minor suits, usually lead the major.
- Consider not leading suits bid or rebid by the opponents.

#1

North

♠J52

♥KQJ8

♦932

♣1086

West (Dealer)

♠AK10

♥1075

♦AKQ

♣9532

East

♠873

♥A93

♦754

♣AKQ4

South

♠Q964

♥642

♦J1086

♣J7

West is the dealer with _____points and bids_____; North passes; East with _____points bids_____; All Pass. What is the contract_____? Who is the declarer_____? Who leads the first card_____? What is the lead___?

#2

North

♠J1063

♥842

♦AJ96

♣A10

West

♠Q74

♥J53

♦K104

♣Q754

East

♠52

♥K1076

♦Q732

♣J83

South (Dealer)

♠AK98

♥AQ9

♦85

♣K962

South is the dealer with _____points and bids ____; West passes; North with _____points bids_____; East passes; South bids_____; West passes; North bids_____; All Pass. What is the contract_____? Who is the declarer_____? Who leads the first card_____? What is the lead___?

#3

North
♠KJ54
♥A10
♦KQ84
♣A64

West
♠A1073
♥643
♦632
♣KJ7

East
♠Q96
♥Q987
♦J95
♣532

South (Dealer)
♠82
♥KJ52
♦A107
♣Q1098

South is the dealer and passes; West passes; North with _____points bids_____; East passes; South bids_____; West passes; North bids____; East passes; South bids____; All Pass. What is the contract____? Who is the declarer____? Who leads the first card____? What is the lead___?

#4

North (Dealer)
♠A93
♥AK3
♦A72
♣Q974

West
♠Q875
♥QJ62
♦Q86
♣K8

East
♠J106
♥1075
♦KJ95
♣J32

South
♠K42
♥984
♦1043
♣A1065

North is the dealer with _____points and bids ____; All Pass. What is the contract____? Who is the declarer____? Who leads the first card____? What is the lead___?

#5

North
♠764
♥A982
♦AK87
♣42

West
♠J109
♥764
♦952
♣Q1093

East
♠Q8532
♥K5
♦QJ10
♣J65

South (Dealer)
♠AK
♥QJ103
♦643
♣AK87

South is the dealer with _____points and bids ____; West passes; North with _____points bids_____; East passes; South bids____; West passes; North bids____; All Pass. What is the contract____? Who is the declarer____? Who leads the first card____? What is the lead___?

#6

North
♠J642
♥Q64
♦K109
♣K42

West
♠AQ107
♥1082
♦QJ6
♣753

East
♠K53
♥J97
♦7432
♣J98

South (Dealer)
♠98
♥AK53
♦A85
♣AQ106

South is the dealer with _____points and bids ____; West passes; North with ____points bids____; East passes; South bids____; All Pass. What is the contract____? Who is the declarer____? Who leads the first card____? What is the lead___?

#7

North
♠KJ7
♥42
♦9653
♣A954

West (Dealer)
♠AQ83
♥J107
♦AJ87
♣K8

East
♠642
♥AQ5
♦Q2
♣Q10732

South
♠1095
♥K9863
♦K104
♣J6

West is the dealer with ____points and bids____; North passes; East with ____points bids____; All Pass. What is the contract____? Who is the declarer____? Who leads the first card____? What is the lead___?

#8

North (Dealer)
♠K103
♥AK73
♦K97
♣A102

West
♠Q42
♥1052
♦AJ65
♣K65

East
♠J9765
♥J9
♦Q82
♣974

South
♠A8
♥Q864
♦1043
♣QJ83

North is the dealer with ____points and bids ____; East passes; South with ____points bids____; West passes; North bids____; East passes; South bids____; All Pass.
What is the contract____? Who is the declarer____? Who leads the first card____?
What is the lead___?

#9

North
♠642
♥Q642
♦K109
♣K42

West
♠A87
♥K875
♦J3
♣A987

East (Dealer)
♠KJ109
♥A3
♦AQ82
♣Q106

South
♠Q53
♥J109
♦7654
♣J53

East is the dealer with ____points and bids ____; South passes; West with ____points bids____; North passes; East bids____; South passes; West bids ____; All Pass. What is the contract____? Who is the declarer____? Who leads the first card____? What is the lead___?

#10

North (Dealer)
♠QJ9
♥AQJ4
♦A53
♣Q42

West
♠K5
♥K106
♦K874
♣10953

East
♠A1087
♥8752
♦102
♣A86

South
♠6432
♥93
♦QJ96
♣KJ7

North is the dealer with ____points and bids ____; All Pass. What is the contract____? Who is the declarer____? Who leads the first card____? What is the lead___?

83

Answers to practice hands on pages 79-83.

#1
West is the dealer with 16 points and bids 1NT; East with 13 points bids 3NT; All Pass.
What is the contract? 3NT. Who is the declarer? West. Who leads the first card? North.
What is the lead? ♥K.

- **Hearing partner's opening 1NT bid (15-17 points), East with 13 points, counts opener's minimum of 15 points, and knows there is enough points for game. 15+13=28 points. East jumps to 3NT. The "one who knows - goes".**

- **North leads ♥K - top of the three-card sequence. Declarer has only one stopper in the heart suit and does not play the ♥A for one round of play of the suit.**

- **After playing the ♥A, West counts nine winners in both his hand and dummy, and plays all his winners making the 3NT contract with an overtrick.**

#2
South is the dealer with 16 points and bids 1NT; North with 10 points bids 2♣ (Stayman); South
bids 2♠; West passes; North bids 4♠; All Pass. What is the contract? 4♠. Who is the declarer?
South. Who leads the first card? West. What is the lead? ♣4 – from West's longest suit..

- **Hearing partner's opening 1NT bid (15-17 points), North with 10 points, and opener's minimum of 15 points, knows there will be game in either a notrump or a suit contract. 10+15=25 points for game.**

- **North first explores a suit contract by bidding 2♣ (Stayman) asking partner major. South bids two spades, and North knows there is an eight-card spade fit, and bids 4♠.**

#3
South is the dealer and passes; North with 17 points bids 1NT; South with 10 points bids 2♣
(Stayman); North bids 2♠, South bids 3NT; All Pass. What is the contract? 3NT.
Who is the declarer? North. Who leads the first card? East. What is the lead? ♥7.

- **Hearing partner's opening 1NT bid (15-17 points), South with 10 points, and opener's minimum of 15 points, knows there will be game in either a notrump or a suit contract. 10+15=25 points for game.**
  South bids 2♣ (Stayman), asking partner for his four-card major.

- **North bids 2♠, which denies the heart suit as North bids the major suits "up the line". South knows North does not have four hearts, and jumps to the 3NT game.**

#4

North is the dealer with 17 points and bids 1NT; All Pass. What is the contract? 1NT. Who is the declarer? North. Who leads the first card? East. What is the lead? ♦ 5.

- **South passes with only seven points.**

- **South does not have the <u>nine points</u> necessary to "invite" partner to game.**

#5

South is the dealer with 17 points and bids 1NT; North with 11 points bids 2♣; South bids 2♥; North bids 4♥; All Pass. What is the contract? 4♥. Who is the declarer? South. Who leads the first card? West. What is the lead? ♠J – top of a three-card sequence.

- **After partner's opening 1NT bid, North with 11 points, knows there will be game in either a notrump or a suit contract. 11+15=26 points for game.**

- **North first explores a suit contract by bidding 2♣ (Stayman), asking partner for his four-card major. South bids 2♥ and now North knows there is an 8-card heart fit, and bids the 4♥ game.**

- **After winning the opening ♠J lead, South leads the ♥Q to finesse West for the ♥K. The finesses loses to East, who leads a ♣J trying to trap And honor in declarer's hand and also <u>through weakness</u> in the dummy, a good defender play. East hopes to promote a trick for partner in the club suit.**

- **Declarer decides to delay drawing trumps, as he must trump two club losers with dummy's higher trumps (98) after playing the ♣AK. East cannot overtrump.**

#6

South is the dealer with 17 points and bids 1NT; North with 9 points and holding a 4-3-3-3 balanced hand bids 2NT invitational; South bids 3NT; All Pass. What is the contract? 3NT. Who is declarer? South. Who leads first card? West.
What is the lead? ♠7.

- **North makes an invitational bid in response to partner's 1NT opening bid.**

- **North will ignore the four-card spade major holding a 4-3-3-3 balanced hand, which offers no ruffing value.**

- **South with the top of his 15-17 range, bids the 3NT game.**

#7

West is the dealer with 15 points and bids 1NT; North passes; East with 11 points bids 3NT. All Pass. What is the contract? 3NT. Who is the declarer? West. Who leads the first card? North. What is the lead? ♣4.

- **North leads fourth card down in his longest and strongest suit... clubs.**

- **Declarer wins in hand, taking the ♣J with the ♣K, and leads the ♥J to the ♥5 in dummy to finesse North for the ♥K - the finesse loses.**

- **South sees the long club suit in dummy and switches to the ♠10 leading up to the spade "weakness" in dummy. Declarer plays the ♠A, forgoing the finesse, and leads a club toward the ♣Q in dummy. North plays the ♣A, and with no better lead, plays a heart.**

- **Declarer takes the ♥A and plays the ♦Q to finesse South for the ♦K. South covers the ♦Q with the king to promote his ♦10.**

- **If South doesn't cover, declarer repeats the diamond finesse. It's important to start the finesse from the hand where you want to repeat the finesse.**

- **Declarer makes three club tricks, three diamond tricks, two heart tricks and a spade trick to make his 3NT contract.**

#8

East and West pass throughout. North is the dealer with 17 points and bids 1NT; East passes; South with 9 points bids 2♣ (Stayman); West passes; North bids 2♥; East passes; South bids 4♥; All Pass. What is the contract? 4♥. Who is the declarer? North. Who leads the first card? East. What is the lead? ♠6 - fourth card down in is longest suit.

- **South with 9 points bids Stayman asking partner for his four-card major.**

- **North bids hearts, and South knows the partnership has an eight-card heart fit and can re-evaluate his hand to 10 points, one extra point for the doubleton spade.**

- **1NT 15-17 points – partner with 10 points = at least 25 points for game, and South bids the 4♥.**

#9

East is the dealer with 16 points and bids 1NT; West with 12 points bids 2♣ (Stayman); East bids 2♠; South passes; West bids 3NT; All Pass.
What is the contract? 3NT. Who is the declarer? East. Who leads the first card? South.
What is the lead? ♥J - top of a sequence.

- **West knows there is a possible game in hearts or 3NT.West bids Stayman to explore 4-4 fit in the heart suit.East bids 2♠, <u>by-passing the heart suit.</u> Opener can't hold four hearts, as he would bid his major suits "up-the-line" with both majors, bidding the heart suit first.**

- **West bids the 3NT game, knowing there is no major suit fit with partner. Declarer wins with the ♥J lead with the ♥A. Declarer plays a low club to the ♣A in dummy, then a low club back to the ♣Q in his hand. This "finesse" play is best <u>if missing the ♣J.</u>**

- **Declarer is hoping North has the ♣K, and the ♣Q wins the trick. Declarer plays the ♠K, then the ♠J - covered by South's ♠Q. Declarer plays dummy's ♠A. The finesse has won.**

- **Declarer leads the ♦J from dummy, covered by North's ♦K to promote his ♦10. North will cover an "honor with an honor" as he wants to promote his ♦10 to be a good trick. North's ♦10 wins a trick. Declarer loses a heart, diamond and a club to make ten tricks and an overtrick in the 3NT contract.**

#10

North is the dealer with 16 points opens the bidding 1NT. All Pass.
What is the contract? 1NT. Who is the declarer? North. Who leads the first card? East.
What is the lead? ♠7.

- **South passes, as he has only seven points, needing at least eight points to bid Staymand or nine points to bid 2NT as an invitation to the 3NT game.**

- **Defenders play three rounds of spades; declarer winning the ♠Q. Declarer leads a low club to the ♣J in dummy, which wins the trick.**

- **Declarer leads the ♦Q, finessing West for the ♦K, winning the trick, Declarer continues the finesse. West does not cover with four diamonds. Declarer reaches dummy with the ♣K to finesse West for the ♥K.**

- **Declarer wins one spade, three diamonds, two clubs and two hearts making an overtrick in his 1NT contract.**

NOTES

GENERAL PLAY   *THE FINESSE PART TWO*

Declarer plans the play of the hand after the opening lead, before playing to the first trick. Playing a card too quickly to the first trick can lead to the defeat of the contract.

Counting tricks:

Declarer Counts losing tricks in a suit contract:
- Count losing tricks in a suit contract, and plan to discard or sluff losing tricks on a long side suit, or trump losers when void in the suit.

Declarer Counts winning tricks in a notrump contract:
- Count winning tricks in a notrump contract such aces, aces and kings in the same suit, and running suits such as AKQJ. After counting winners, determine how many additional tricks are needed to fulfill the contract.

Play suggestions: Make **extra trump tricks**
- You can make "extra" trump tricks by using dummy's trumps, called "trumping on the short side" or dummy side of the trump suit.

Why? Declarer will usually make the small cards in a long suit by force, such as AKQxxx in declarer's hand. Trumping in the long hand may not produce extra tricks.

Count cards: Declarer and defenders should both count cards.

- A good way to remember how many cards are played in the trump suit, is by saying to yourself "that's four" when the suit is played once, or "eight" the second time the suit is played. Add the cards played to the remaining cards in your hand and in the dummy, and subtract the number from 13. You will know how many cards are still outstanding.

- It's important to notice if all players have followed suit when the suit is played. For example, when drawing spade trumps, and an opponent discards a club. If you don't pay attention to all the cards played, you may think it's a spade.

- It's important to count cards in suits other than the trump suit. If the AK is played in a suit and you have the queen, remind yourself that the queen is now a good trick.

- If the suit has been played three times and all players have followed suit, be reminded that the outstanding 13th card is good. Honors are easy to identify early, however it's important to identify for example a 9 or 8 spot card. For example, you finesse up to the AQ, playing the Q - LHO plays the 10, and Q loses to the K. Winning the return, you next play the A dropping the J. You have the 98 - they're good - identify it. Remember the spot cards - very important!

The preference bid or pass:

Many contracts should stop at low levels when you have only a seven-card trump fit. Frequently, there doesn't seem to be a better contract with the combined hands.

West			East
♠87	1♥	1♠	♠AQ95
♥AQJ86	2♣	2♥	♥72
♦K3	Pass		♦J10542
♣KQ54			♣102

When in doubt, weak hands should take a preference for partner's first bid suit if possible.

- West opens 1♥. East with 8 points bids 1♠, a forcing bid by a non-passed hand.
- West can't repeat his five-card heart suit, as he needs six to rebid his <u>unsupported</u> suit, and bids 2♣, his second suit.
- East bids 2♥. East has taken a preference for partner's first bid suit with a <u>weak hand</u>.
- East did not support West's heart suit immediately which would show a 3+card raise, so the 2♥ rebid merely shows a preference to partner's first bid suit and a weak hand.
- The contract will play in a seven-card fit. With no other choice of contracts, seven-card fits can be bid at low levels. West will pass.
- East could also pass partner's 2♣ bid if East strongly preferred the club suit.
- In the above sample hand, East could not bid 2♦ or 2NT without 10+points.

Defenders:

- The goal of the defenders is to defeat the contract.
- The LHO of the declarer leads the first card, and the choice of first leads is often the most important decision made in defense of the contract.
- The lead decision is based on bids made by partner and the opponents.

Cover an Honor with an Honor:

- A general point of defense is that it is usually correct to cover opponent's honor with an honor, unless you can see the J or 10 in dummy.

    Why? You hope to knock out high cards from the opponent's hand to promote lower cards such as the J and 10 in your hand or partner's hand.

Giving a Ruff and Sluff: Usually a bad defender play.

- If a defender knows both declarer and dummy are void in the same suit, a lead of the suit may give declarer a "ruff" in one hand and a "sluff" of a loser in the other hand.

Suggested leads during play of the hand:

When in doubt, left hand opponent (LHO) of declarer should lead "through strength" in dummy.

Why: When LHO of declarer leads through strength in dummy, the lead may allow partner to play a higher card than dummy and win the trick, or force an even higher trick from declarer to set up an honor for the defense. You are also less likely to surrender one of your own honors.

When in doubt, right hand opponent (RHO) of declarer should lead the "weak suit" in dummy.

Why: RHO of declarer should not lead into a strong suit in dummy as dummy plays last and may trap partner's high cards or your own.

RHO should lead the weak suit in dummy, through strength in declarer's hand, allowing partner to play after the declarer plays and capture his honors.

Table play: Generally second hand plays low - third hand plays high.

Second hand low:

- When a low card has been played, and you are second hand to play to a trick, you will generally play a low card if you can't win the trick.

  Why: As partner is the last to play, playing second hand low may force declarer to play a high card from his hand or dummy to try to win the trick.

  Partner may then be able to play a higher card than the declarer and win the trick, and you save your own honors for when you may need them.

Third hand high:

- When you are third hand to play to a trick, play a high card either to win the trick or to force out an opponents' higher card. However, if partner has led a high card you usually don't want to play another high card. Playing a high card may force declarer to play a higher and promote a winner for partner.

  Why: If a low card is led by partner, playing third hand high after the dummy plays a low card may set up a high card in partner's hand. Also, it doesn't give declarer a "cheap" trick with a low card, declarer being the last to play to the trick.

  Example. Partner leads ♠2 dummy ♠5 you -third hand ♠Q declarer ♠A. Partner led low from an honor – ♠K now a good trick.

THE FINESSE PART TWO

As we learned in Chapter 3, the "finesse" is a form of declarer play of taking tricks by capturing an opponent's honor between declarer's lower and higher honors.

- The finesse allows you to make extra tricks by capturing opponent's honors.
- When you finesse, you play one defender for a certain card holding
- A good way to know if you should finesse is to ask yourself how it would help you if your opponent covers your honor with their honor.

Do not finesse by leading the queen unless you also have the jack in the suit:

Example: **Dummy**   **Declarer**
        A8762   Q54**3**

- Lead the three from your hand toward the ace in dummy. Then play the two in dummy towards the queen in your hand, playing your RHO for the king. By this route you will lose only one trick, unless the king is twice guarded over the queen – then there is nothing you could do. For reference purposes, consider why leading the queen cannot work; you would lose two tricks to your RHO's holding KJ10, by contrast, leading the ace then back toward your queen loses just one trick.

Finesse by leading towards double honors:

Why? If declarer leads a low spade towards the ♠KQ2 in dummy, Declarer's LHO may play the ♠A, and declarer will play dummy's ♠2. The ♠KQ will now be good tricks. If LHO does **not** play the ♠A, declarer plays the ♠K, and returns to his hand to lead another low card toward dummy's ♠Q. Always lead toward the card you hope will win the trick. This way you lose a trick to the ace but score two tricks in return.

Defense of the finesse:

- A commonly used phrase in Bridge is to "cover an honor with an honor".
- Only cover an honor with an honor if it will promote a trick in partner's hand or in your hand. For example you may cover the queen with the king and build the nine or ten of the suit into an eventual winner.
- Do not cover the honor when the J109 are exposed in the dummy, as there is no card to promote for the defense. Usually cover the second honor played from dummy, not the first.

Examples:

Dummy leads ♠QJ108	You hold ♠K32	Don't cover, nothing to promote.
Dummy leads ♠Q985	You hold ♠K103	Cover with your king, promote 10.
Dummy leads ♠QJ98	You hold ♠K103	Don't cover Q, cover J, promote 10.

Declarer leads ♠J to dummy's ♠A864	You hold ♠Q84. Play low, declarer may hold KJ10 and play dummy's Ace to finesse back to his hand, your ♠Q winning.
Declarer leads ♠Q to dummy's ♠AJ6	You hold ♠K107. Play the ♠K, promote 10.
Declarer leads ♠5 to dummy's ♠AK109	Holding ♠QJ64. Don't split honors, play low.

Sample finesse hand: Contract: 4♠   West leads ♣10

Bidding:

South (Dealer)	West	North	East
1♣	Pass	1♥	Pass
1♠	Pass	4♠	All Pass

North
♠QJ54
♥A942
♦AQ8
♣J5

West
♠K6
♥K103
♦K95
♣<u>10</u>9832

East
♠982
♥J87
♦10643
♣Q64

South (Dealer)
♠A1073
♥Q65
♦J72
♣AK7

- South with 14 points and no five-card major bids 1♣. North with 14 points bids 1♥, bidding his major suits "up the line." North's new suit is a forcing bid, South rebids 1♠. North knows there is at least an 8-card spade fit; adding South's 12+opening points to his 14 points arrives at 26 points and the 4♠ game. A common Bridge saying is "The one who knows goes!"

- South sees two possible heart losers, a spade loser and club loser. Declarer can finesse the ♠K, K♥ and♦K. Declarer plays the ♣J from dummy, East covers with the queen, and South plays the ♣AK, and trumps the club loser in dummy. No club loser.

- Declarer plays dummy's ♠Q, East the ♠2 and declarer the ♠3, West wins ♠K. After losing the spade finesse, South draws the trumps.

- Declarer begins the diamond finesse by leading the ♦J from his hand. West covers the ♦J with the ♦K. The finesses is successful, however, West's covering the ♦J with his ♦K, promotes the ♦10 in the East hand.

- South plays to the ♥A in dummy, and a small heart toward the ♥Q in his hand, playing East for ♥K which loses to West.

- South loses three tricks, making the 4♠ contract.

Dummy	Declarer	Finesse combinations
AK2	**J**106	Lead the jack, and if it wins there are no losers in the suit.
A73	**Q**J10	Lead the queen, and if it wins, repeat the finesse with the jack.
KJ10	87**2**	Lead low and play the 10 in dummy if LHO plays low. If the 10 loses to the ace, return to your hand and lead low to the jack, playing LHO for the queen.
AQ75	**J**106	Lead the jack and if the jack wins, repeat the finesse by leading the 10.
AJ10	98**6**	Lead low and play the 10 if LHO plays low. If the 10 loses to either the king or queen, return to your hand and play low to the jack, finesse the king.
K76	**J**108	Lead the jack and play low if LHO plays low; if the jack loses to the ace, return to your hand and repeat the finesse.
Q94	**A**32	Play the ace, then play low towards the queen. DON'T lead the queen!
AQ10	84**2**	Lead low toward the 10, then return to your hand and finesse the queen, hoping North has the king.
AQJ109	**8**	This is a variant of a finesse, called a ruffing finesse, and it applies only when you have a side-suit like this at a trump contract. Lead the 8 to the ace and then lead the queen, hoping your RHO has the king. If RHO covers your queen with the king, you ruff and if not, you discard a loser from your hand
KQJ107	---	Ruffing finesse: Lead the king from dummy, hoping North has the ace, and if it is covered, ruff. If RHO doesn't cover, discard a loser from your hand,
A65	Q**10**9	Lead the 10, play low from dummy when LHO plays low. If the 10 loses to the jack, lead the queen to finesse LHO for the king.
KQ65	74**3**	Lead the three from your hand, playing your LHO for the ace. If your king wins the trick, return to your hand to play a low card toward the queen.
AJ53	**K**876	With an 8-card fit, the queen will not usually fall. Finesse LHO for the queen, playing the king first, and then finessing the jack. A general rule in Bridge is with "eight cards ever, nine cards never" as to whether to finesse for the queen. With nine cards, you hope to drop the queen.
A754	**J**1098	This is a double finesse since you are two missing honors. Lead the jack an if LHO plays low, play low from dummy. If RHO plays an honor, next play the 10 and finesse LHO for the other honor.
AQ65	**10**984	Lead the 10 and led it ride. Repeat the finesse next by leading the 9 through the AQ.

Answers on page 97.

#1

North (Dealer)
♠Q52
♥63
♦AK65
♣A1082

West
♠987
♥AQ952
♦109
♣543

East
♠J106
♥874
♦QJ832
♣Q6

South
♠AK43
♥KJ10
♦74
♣KJ97

North is the dealer with _____points and bids____; East passes; South with ____points bids____; West passes; North bids____; East passes; South bids____; All Pass. What is the contract____? Who is the declarer____? Who leads the first card____? What is the lead___?

#2

North
♠86
♥K1095
♦K832
♣K107

West
♠KJ103
♥62
♦A109
♣Q982

East
♠Q9542
♥J3
♦QJ54
♣65

South (Dealer)
♠A7
♥AQ874
♦76
♣AJ43

South is the dealer with _____points and bids____; West passes; North with ____points bids____; East passes; South bids____; All Pass. What is the contract____? Who is the declarer____? Who leads the first card____? What is the lead___?

#3

North (Dealer)
♠A
♥K732
♦K765
♣AQ87

West
♠KQ109
♥Q54
♦104
♣5432

East
♠J5432
♥6
♦A983
♣KJ9

South
♠876
♥AJ1098
♦QJ2
♣106

North is the dealer with _____points and bids____; East passes; South with ____points bids____; West passes; North bids____; East passes; South bids____; All Pass. What is the contract____? Who is the declarer____? Who leads the first card____? What is the lead___?

#4

North (Dealer)
♠AK108
♥J2
♦108
♣AQJ52

West
♠97
♥K98
♦A976
♣K1063

East
♠J63
♥7543
♦KJ52
♣87

South
♠Q542
♥AQ106
♦Q43
♣94

North is the dealer with ___points and bids____; East passes; South with ___points bids____; West passes; North bids____; East passes; South bids____; West passes; North bids____; East passes; South bids____; All Pass. What is the contract____? Who is the declarer____? Who leads the first card____? What is the lead___?

🕵 Answers to practice hands on pages 95-96.

#1. North is the dealer with 13 points and bids 1♦; East passes; South with 15 points bids 1♠; West passes; North bids 2♣; South bids 3NT; All Pass. What is the contract? 3NT. Who is the declarer? South. Who leads the first card? West. What is the lead? ♥5 - fourth card down in longest and strongest suit. South wins with the ♥10.

- **Key Play: South has a two-way finesse for the ♣Q. Declarer plays dummy's ♣2 to the ♣J in his hand, (playing East for the ♣Q) into the West's "safe" hand.**
- **The play does not endanger South's ♥KJ, for a finesse into the East hand, the "danger" hand, allows East to lead a heart THROUGH South's ♥KJ losing to West's ♥AQ. West will play heart tricks and the contract will fail.**

#2 South is the dealer with 16 points and bids 1♥; West passes; North with 10 points (one point for the doubleton spade) jumps to 3♥; East passes; South bids 4♥; West passes; All Pass. What is the contract? 4♥. Who is the declarer? South. Who leads the first card? West. What is the lead? ♠J- top of interior sequence.

- **Declarer wins the ♠A and draws trumps. Declarer plays the ♣J from his hand and hopes West covers the ♣J with the ♣Q. West sees the ♣10 in dummy and does not cover the ♣J. Subsequently, South leads a low diamond up to the ♦K in the dummy, playing West for the ♦A. Both finesses are successful.**

#3 North is the dealer with 16 points and bids 1♦; East passes; South with 9 points bids 1♥; West passes; North jumps to 3♥ with 18 points by adding two points for the singleton ♠A. East passes; South bids 4♥; All Pass. What is the contract? 4♥. Who is the declarer? South. Who leads the first card? West. What is the lead? ♠K - top of sequence lead.

- **After winning the ♠A in dummy, a low diamond is led from dummy to declarer's ♦Q, playing East for the ♦A. East plays low. Declarer ruffs a spade in the dummy, and leads a heart to the ♥A in his hand, and ruffs his last spade in the dummy, and plays dummy's ♥K. Declarer now plays a low diamond to his ♦J. East takes his ♦A, but must lead away from his ♣K as spade lead provides declarer with a ruff and sluff of a losing club. A diamond lead enables declarer to sluff a losing club on the good ♦K in dummy.**

#4 North is the dealer with 16 points and bids 1♣; East passes; South with 10 points bids 1♥; West passes; North bids 1♠; East passes; South bids 2♠ promising four spades; West passes. North now with 17 points jumps to 3♠- invitational. North added one point for the doubleton diamond, and no extra points for the doubleton heart as the ♥J was counted, East passes; South bids 4♠; All Pass. What is the contract? 4♠. Who is the declarer? North. Who leads the first card? East. What is the lead? ♦2 - low from an honor.

- **South has two suits to finesse. One for the ♥K by playing the ♥J to dummy's ♥AQ (losing to the ♥K). The second finesse is to play a low club from dummy toward his ♣AQ, winning the finesse against West ♣K. Declarer will lose two diamond tricks and one heart trick, 4♠ contract made.**

CHAPTER SIX
THE BOTTOM LINE

General Play:
- Declarer counts losing tricks in a suit contract.
- Declarer counts winning tricks in a NT contract.
- Try to return partner's opening lead suit most of the time, especially in a notrump contract.
- You can make extra trump tricks by using dummy's trumps, called trumping on the "short side" of the trump suit.
- A good way to remember how many cards are played in a suit is by saying "that's four" when the suit is played once, or "that's eight" the second time the suit is played. Add the number of trumps played to the remaining trumps in your hand and dummy's hand and subtract from 13 to know how many trumps are still outstanding.

Suggested Leads During Play of the Hand:
- Left hand opponent (LHO) of declarer should lead through strength in dummy.
- Right hand opponent (RHO) of declarer should lead the weak suit in dummy.

The Preference Bid or Pass:
- Weak hands should take a preference for partner's first bid suit. when practical (holding at least two cards without a marked liking for the second suit).

Table Play:
- Second hand plays low. When a low card is played from dummy, you usually play a low card when you are second hand to play.
- Third hand plays high. If partner leads a low card, and dummy plays a low card, and you are the third hand to play; you will usually play a high card to force the last player to play an even higher card, which may promote a trick for partner.

Defense of the Contract:
- The goal of the defenders is to defeat the contract won by the declarer and his partner. The LHO of the declarer leads the first card, and the choice of first leads is often the most important decision made in defense of the contract. The lead decision is based on bids made by partner and the opponents, and lead guidelines in lesson two.

Giving a Ruff and Sluff: A bad Defender play
- If a defender knows both declarer and dummy are void in the same suit, a lead of that suit may give declarer a ruff in one hand and a sluff of a loser in the other hand.

The Finesse:
- The "finesse" is a form of declarer play of taking tricks by capturing an opponent's honor between declarer's lower and higher honors, or leading toward the card you hope to win.

CHAPTER SEVEN

 *OVERCALLS*  *TAKEOUT DOUBLES*

Overcalls:

When your RHO opens the bidding it's important to "overcall" with a <u>good five+card suit</u> suit and moderate or better values in order to compete with the opponents. You may also make a 1NT overcall over your RHO's suit with 15-18 points, and at least one good stopper in your RHO's suit. If it applies, responder can bid Stayman after partner's 1NT overcall.

Why overcall?

- You've introduced a suit for partner to lead if the opponents win the contract, and partner is on lead.
- You may find a game or part-score, or you may push the opponents too high in the bidding.
- You may also want to make a "sacrifice" bid. A sacrifice is a competitive bid that may not be successful. However, your sacrifice bid may be less costly than allowing the opponents to make their contract, especially if they are vulnerable and you are non-vulnerable.

Overcall requirements:

- Overcall your RHO's opening bid with a <u>good five+card suit.</u>
- Don't overcall with a four-card suit unless you have opening values, the suit is very strong and includes three of the top four cards.
- Overcalls on the one-level may have less than an opening hand.
- Overcalls at the two-level require at least a five+card suit and an opening hand of 12+points.

Good suits: AK1087, AQ654, AJ987, KQJ65, KQ1097, KJ1086, QJ1086

Overcalls at the one-level: 8+points.

- As you may overcall with as few as 8 points, you must have a good five+card suit because your partner will probably lead your suit if you defend the contract.

Overcalls at the two-level: 12+points.

- You need at least an opening hand and a good five-card suit to overcall at the two-level, since partner must go to the three-level to support your suit.

Responses to partner's overcalls:

- Responses in new suits to one-level overcalls are non-forcing but encouraging.
- When partner is an overcaller on the one-level, responder needs slightly higher points to respond to partner's one-level overcall, than to a two-level overcall.
- Respond to two-level overcalls as if partner made an opening bid promising 12-16 points and a five+card suit.
- Responder bids game with support for the two-level overcall suit and game values.
- With no support for partner's overcall suit and 17+points, responder can "cuebid" the opponent's suit to show a strong hand asking the overcaller to bid again.
- A cuebid is an artificial bid to show values, and is forcing overcaller to bid again.

Responses to partner's overcalls
with support In partner's suit.

One-level overcalls:

7-10 points: Raise to the two-level.
11-14 points: Jump to the three-level.
15-16 points: Raise to game level.
17+points: Cuebid opponent's suit, forcing bid.

Two-level overcalls:

8 -11 points: Raise to the three-level.
12+16 points: Bid game.
17+points: Cuebid opponent's suit.

Responder's bids to partner's overcalls
without support In partner's suit

One-level overcalls:

8+12 points: Bid a new suit at the one-level with a good five+card suit
13-15 points: Jump in a new suit at the two-level and a good five+card suit.
17+points: Cuebid opponent's suit.

Responder's notrump bids *without support* in partner's suit
and a stopper in his LHO opponent's opening suit

8-11 points: Bid 1NT.
12-14 points: Bid 2NT.
15-16 points: Bid 3NT.

Sample overcall hand: Contract 4♠   East leads the ♥A
Bidding:

West (Dealer)	North	East	South
1♥	1♠ (overcall)	2♥	4♠ (game)
All Pass			

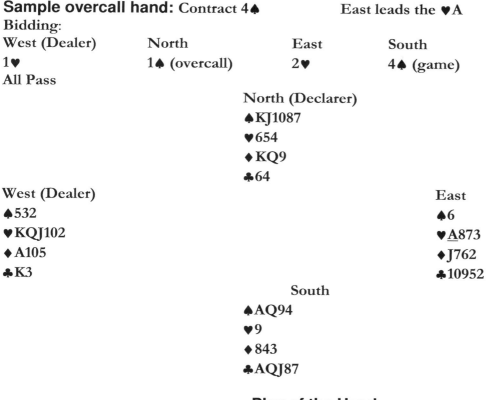

North (Declarer)
♠KJ1087
♥654
♦KQ9
♣64

West (Dealer)
♠532
♥KQJ102
♦A105
♣K3

East
♠6
♥A873
♦J762
♣10952

South
♠AQ94
♥9
♦843
♣AQJ87

Play of the Hand

Declarer must make a game plan after the first lead of the ♥A when and dummy is tabled. Declarer will count how many <u>losing tricks</u> in declarer's hand. Declarer counts three possible heart losers, one or two diamond losers, and a club loser. Declarer can avoid two heart losers by trumping hearts in the dummy.

- East leads the ♥A, dummy plays the ♥9, West the ♥2, North follows with the ♥4. East is on lead. With no more hearts in the dummy, East switches to low spade to shorten dummy's trumps. Declarer knows he must use the trumps in the dummy (the short side of the trump suit) to trump losing hearts before pulling defender's trumps.

- Declarer wins the spade lead in his hand, and trumps a low heart in the dummy. Declarer leads a low diamond to the ♦KQ in his hand (playing up toward honors). West plays low and North plays the ♦K. The ♦K wins the trick, and declarer knows West has the ♦A, as East did not capture the ♦K with the ♦A.

- Declarer trumps his last heart in dummy, draws trumps, and leads a diamond from dummy to the ♦Q in his hand. West decides to play his ♦A and leads a third heart. Declarer wins in his hand, and plays the ♣4 to the ♣Q in dummy losing to West ♣K.

- Declarer makes five trump tricks in his hand, two heart ruffs in dummy, the ♦KQ and the ♣A. Ten tricks made in the 4♠ contract.

#1   North
                                          ♠KJ1087
                                          ♥K104
                                          ♦109
                                          ♣K64

West (Dealer)   East
♠63   ♠94
♥92   ♥J753
♦AKQ785   ♦J643
♣A108   ♣J92

                                          South
                                          ♠AQ52
                                          ♥AQ86
                                          ♦2
                                          ♣Q753

West is the dealer with _____ points and bids _____; North with _____ points bids _____; East passes;
South with _____ points bids _____; All Pass. What is the contract _____? Who is the declarer _____?
Who leads the first card _____? What is the lead _____?

#2   North
                                          ♠9
                                          ♥AKJ542
                                          ♦J95
                                          ♣Q98

West (Dealer)   East
♠AKQJ76   ♠8432
♥963   ♥10
♦K10   ♦Q82
♣J4   ♣A10532

                                          South
                                          ♠105
                                          ♥Q87
                                          ♦A7643
                                          ♣K76

West is the dealer with _____ points and bids _____; North with _____ points bids _____;
East with _____ points bids _____; South passes; West bids _____; All Pass.
What is the contract _____? Who is the declarer _____? Who leads the first card _____?
What is the lead _____?

#3

North
♠KQ7
♥K652
♦AK6
♣Q43

West (Dealer)
♠AJ984
♥843
♦1072
♣AK

East
♠652
♥J7
♦985
♣J8765

South
♠103
♥AQ109
♦QJ43
♣1092

West is the dealer with _____points and bids _____; North with _____points bids_____; East passes; South with _____points bids_____; West passes; North bids_____; East passes; South bids_____; All Pass. What is the contract_____? Who is the declarer_____? Who leads the first card_____? What is the lead___?

#4

North
♠Q653
♥8632
♦109
♣AK4

West
♠K92
♥Q1095
♦AJ6
♣875

East (Dealer)
♠8
♥AKJ74
♦Q873
♣QJ6

South
♠AJ1074
♥---
♦K542
♣10932

East is the dealer with _____points and bids___; South overcalls _____; West with _____points bids_____; North with ___points _____bids _____; East bids_____; All Pass. What is the contract_____? Who is the declarer_____? Who leads the first card_____? What is the lead___?

#5

North (Dealer)
♠K104
♥854
♦AQ984
♣A4

West
♠QJ9
♥AJ6
♦632
♣Q873

East
♠A863
♥KQ2
♦KJ10
♣KJ2

South
♠752
♥10973
♦75
♣10965

North is the dealer with _____points and bids____; East overcalls ____; South passes;
West with _____points bids____; All Pass. What is the contract____? Who is the declarer_____?
Who leads the first card____? What is the lead___?

#6

North
♠Q1072
♥K762
♦Q972
♣7

West
♠A843
♥53
♦53
♣J6543

East (Dealer)
♠K9
♥A1098
♦J10
♣AQ1082

South
♠J65
♥QJ4
♦AK864
♣K9

East is the dealer with _____points and bids___; South overcalls ____; West with___points bids___;
North with points ____bids ____; East bids ____; South passes; West passes; North bids____;
All Pass. What is the contract____? Who is the declarer____? Who leads the first card____?
What is the lead___?

Answers to practice hands on pages 102- 104.

#1

West is the dealer with 15 points and bids 1♦; North with 11 points overcalls 1♠; East passes; South with 16 points jumps to 4♠; All Pass.
What is the contract? 4♠. Who is declarer? North. Who leads the first card? East.
What is the lead? ♦3.

- **North makes an overcall of 1♠. North does not need an opening hand to overcall on the one level, however, North must have a good five-card suit for his overcall.**

- **South reevaluates his hand to 16 points, adding two points for the diamond singleton holding four spades and a fit with partner. South jumps to 4♠ game.**

#2

West is the dealer with 16 points and bids 1♠; North with 15 points overcalls 2♥;
East with 9 points bids 2♠, counting two points for the singleton heart.
South bids 3♥; West bids 3♠ invitational, North passes and East bids 4♠. All Pass.
What is the contract? 4♠. Who is declarer? West. Who leads the first card? North.
What is the lead? ♥A.

- **North overcalls on the two-level with an opening hand and a five-card heart suit, leading the ♥A. Seeing the singleton heart in dummy, North leads a low diamond to South's ♦A.**

- **Declarer loses a heart, club and a diamond to make the 4♠ contract.**

#3

West is the dealer with 13 points and bids 1♠; North with 17 points overcalls 1NT holding stoppers in the spade suit; East passes; South with 9 points bids 2♣ (Stayman); West passes; North bids 2♥; East passes; South adds one point for the doubleton spade and bids 4♥, All Pass.
What is the contract? 4♥. Who is declarer? North. Who leads the first card? East.
What is the lead? ♠2

- **North has a 1NT opening, however, in addition to the point count and balanced hand, North must hold stoppers (♠KQ) in his RHO's opening suit to overcall 1NT.**

#4

East is the dealer with 14 points and bids 1♥; South with 9 points overcalls 1♠; West jumps to 3♥ (a limit raise); North with 10 points and four spades competes to 3♠; East bids 4♥; All Pass. What is the contract? 4♥. Who is declarer? East. Who leads the first card? South. What is the lead? ♠A.

- **South will lead the ♠A, as partner has supported the suit.**

- **East will finesse South for the ♦K, and make his 4♥ contract, losing two clubs and one spade.**

#5

North is the dealer with 14 points and bids 1♦; East with 17 points overcalls 1NT; South passes; West with 10 points bids 3NT; All Pass. What is the contract? 3NT. Who is declarer? East. Who leads the first card? South. What is the lead? ♦7.

- **East with 17 points and stoppers in the diamond suit overcalls 1NT.**
- **After South leads a diamond to North's ♦A, and a diamond is continued, and East must play the ♦J, finessing North for the ♦Q.**

- **Declarer plays the ♣K forcing out the ♣A, and wins the diamond return with the ♦K. Declarer now plays a club to the ♣Q in dummy, and plays the ♠Q to finesse North for the ♠K - the finesse wins.**

- **East does not play the winners in the heart suit, as he will use the suit as a "transportation suit" to allow entries to his hand and to the dummy.**
- **Declarer loses a diamond and a club to make two overtricks in his 3NT contract.**

#6

East is the dealer with 15 points and bids 1♣; South overcalls 1♦; West with 8 points bids 2♣; North with 9 points bids 2♦; East bids 3♣; South passes; West passes; North with four diamonds bids 3♦; All Pass. What is the contract? 3♦. Who is declarer? South. Who leads the first card? West. What is the lead? ♣3.

- **West can re-evaluate his hand to eight points with an extra two points for the heart and diamond doubletons, and one point for length in the club suit.**

- **As South promised at least a five-card diamond suit by his overcall, North re-evaluates his hand two more points for the singleton club to arrive at nine points.**
- **Because of the overcalls, both opponents attempted to bid a part score.**

- **As North competes to the three-level. knowing there is at least a nine-card fit in diamonds. The diamond suit out-ranked the club suit and won the competitive auction.**

 **Takeout Doubles:**

In the past, fifty years ago, any doubles made in the bidding were considered penalty doubles. However, a more frequent use for the double in modern bidding is called a takeout double. This is especially so when the opponents have established a fit in a suit.

A takeout double asks partner to bid his best suit.

- When your RHO opens the bidding, you can make a takeout double to ask partner to bid his best suit.

- In response to your takeout double, partner can also bid notrump with stoppers in the opponent's opening suit.

- Your takeout double is almost never a penalty double of a suit at low-levels.

A takeout double shows an opening hand with 12+points.

- Your takeout double says you have an opening hand, and can support any suit partner bids. You usually promise the other four-card major if your RHO opens a major.

- You don't have a good five+card suit to overcall RHO's opening bid.

- You may count extra points for short suits in your RHO's suit <u>before</u> hearing a fit with partner. You are counting on a presumed fit with partner, called dummy points.

Example: RHO opens 1♥. Make a takeout double with the following hand.

♠KQ98, ♥5, ♦KJ76, ♣QJ54 - 12 HCP + 2 points for the singleton heart = 14 points.

Make a takeout double: You're short in your RHO suit, with no five+card suit to overcall.

Don't make a takeout double with too many cards in your RHO's opening suit:

Holding too many cards in your RHO's opening suit will not give you enough cards in the other three suits to support any suit partner bids.
Example: RHO opens 1♥: You hold: ♠A3 ♥QJ74 ♦K109 ♣K872.

With no other bid, you may have to pass, and hope partner comes into the bidding later in the auction with a suit you can support. If you make a takeout double, partner may bid spades, and you will have given partner misinformation since you've promised support in the unbid suits.

Partner makes a takeout double and your RHO passes - you are forced to bid:

You are forced to bid even with zero points. If you pass, the auction will end, and the opponents may easily make a one-level doubled contract.

Responses to partner's takeout double when your RHO passes.

Suit bids:

0-8 points: Bid suit at cheapest level.
9-11 points: Jump a level in your suit.
12+points: Cuebid the opponent's opening suit, or jump to game in a major.

Example of cuebid: LHO bids 1♥; partner makes a takeout double, and your RHO passes. You cuebid 2♥ to show 12+points and game values*.

*You may pass to convert the takeout double to a penalty double holding at least five+cards and honors in LHO's opening suit.

Notrump bids:

6-10 points, balanced: Bid 1NT with stoppers in opener's suit.
11-12 points, balanced: Jump to 2NT with stoppers in opener's suit.
13-15 points, balanced: Jump to 3NT with stoppers in opener's suit.

Responses to Partner's Takeout Doubles when Your RHO Bids.

Suit bids:

6-9 points: Bid four+card major not bid by opener.
6-9 points: Bid a new suit at the one-level.
10+points: Bid a new suit at the two-level.

Notrump bids:

6-10 points, balanced: Bid 1NT with stoppers in opener's suit.
11-12 points, balanced: Jump to 2NT with stoppers in opener's suit.
13-15 points, balanced: Jump to 3NT with stoppers in opener's suit.

Sample takeout double hand:

Contract: 4♥　　　East leads ♠A
Bidding:

East (Dealer)	South	West	North
1♠	Double	Pass	3♥ (9-11 points)
Pass	4♥	All Pass	

North
♠1064
♥AQ43
♦72
♣QJ98

West
♠Q95
♥852
♦10983
♣654

East (Dealer)
♠AK8732
♥109
♦K54
♣A7

South
♠J
♥KJ76
♦AQJ6
♣K1032

Takeout Doubler:

- Your RHO opens 1♠ and you can support any suit partner bids.
- You have an opening hand, and you are "short" in your RHO opening suit.
- Make a takeout double.

Responder:

- Your RHO passes and you are forced to bid.
- You can show your partner your point count by jumping one-level in your suit.
- Your jump shows 9-11 points and at least a four-card suit.

Takeout Doubler:

- You have a fit in partner's heart suit and your point count is 16 points.
  Adding your partner's minimum 9 points to your 16 points = 25 points.
- You bid the 4♥ game contract.

#1

North
- ♠64
- ♥QJ8
- ♦J98
- ♣Q964

West
- ♠AQ108
- ♥32
- ♦A75
- ♣KJ102

East
- ♠J932
- ♥54
- ♦K1032
- ♣A53

South (Dealer)
- ♠65
- ♥AK10976
- ♦Q64
- ♣87

South is the dealer with _____points and bids____; West with ____points makes a takeout double; North with ____points bids____; East with ____points bids____; South bids____; West bids____; All Pass. What is the contract____? Who is the declarer____? Who leads the first card____? What is the lead____?

#2

North
- ♠KJ54
- ♥1098
- ♦Q32
- ♣A75

West
- ♠73
- ♥743
- ♦J964
- ♣J1032

East (Dealer)
- ♠Q96
- ♥A52
- ♦AK105
- ♣986

South
- ♠A1082
- ♥KQJ6
- ♦87
- ♣KQ4

East is the dealer with _____points and bids____; South with ____points makes a takeout double; West passes; North with ____points bids____; East passes; South bids____. What is the contract____? Who is the declarer____? Who leads the first card____? What is the lead____?

#3

North
♠642
♥1087
♦85432
♣87

West
♠KJ75
♥54
♦KQ10
♣A1065

East
♠AQ93
♥K92
♦J76
♣QJ3

South (Dealer)
♠108
♥AQJ63
♦A9
♣K942

South is the dealer with _____points and bids____; West with ____points makes a takeout double; North passes; East bids____; South passes; West bids____; North passes; East bids____; All Pass. What is the contract____? Who is the declarer____? Who leads the first card____? What is the lead____?

#4

North (Dealer)
♠A53
♥AK872
♦Q94
♣Q4

West
♠J4
♥QJ105
♦QJ2
♣AJ83

East
♠KQ92
♥96
♦AK106
♣K97

South
♠10876
♥43
♦873
♣10652

North is the dealer with _____points and bids____; East makes a takeout double; South passes; West bids____; North passes; East bids____; All Pass. What is the contract____? Who is the declarer____? Who leads the first card____? What is the lead____?

Answers to practice hands on page 110 - 111.

#1 South is the dealer with 14 points and bids 1♥; West with 14 points makes a takeout double; North with six points bids 2♥; East with 8 points bids 2♠; South bids 3♥; West bids 3♠; All Pass. What is the contract? 3♠. Who is the declarer? East. Who leads the first card? South. What is the lead? ♥A.

- **After South's 1♥ opening bid, West makes a takeout double with 14 points, shortness in his RHO'S heart suit, and support for any suit partner bids.**
- **North bids 2♥, East competes to 2♠. South bids 3♥, West competes to 3♠.**
- **West must finesse South for the ♠K to make the contract.**

#2 East is the dealer with 13 points and bids 1♦; South with 15 points makes a takeout double; West passes; North with 10 points jumps to 2♠ (9-11 points); East passes; South now with 16 points bids 4♠; All Pass. What is the contract? 4♠. Who is the declarer? North. Who leads the first card? East. What is the lead? ♦A.

- **South makes a takeout double with shortness in his RHO's suit, and support for any suit partner bids. North is forced to bid and jumps to 2♠ to show a 9-11 point count.**
- **South now holds 16 points, adding an extra point for the doubleton diamond with the spade fit. South bids 4♠. East leads the ♦AK and switches to the ♣9, top of nothing lead. North plays the ♣A, and finesses East for the ♠Q, as East was the opening bidder and should hold most of the high card points.**
- **The finesse is successful, and declarer draws trumps. North loses just the ♦AK and the ♥A, making the 4♠ contract.**

#3 South is the dealer with 15 points and bids 1♥; West with 14 points (+1 point for the doubleton heart) makes a takeout double, North passes; East bids 2♥ to show 12+points; South passes, West bids 2♠. North passes; East bids 4♠; All Pass. West is the declarer in 4♠. North leads the ♥7.

- **Declarer draws trump ending in dummy, to take the club finesse.**

#4 North is the dealer with 16 points and bids 1♥; East makes a takeout double; South passes; West bids 2NT; North passes; East bids 3NT; All Pass. West is the declarer in 3NT. North leads ♥A.

- **West jumps to show an invitational notrump contract with heart stoppers.**
- **North leads the ♥A,♥K and another heart to attempt to set up hearts with ♠A entry.**
- **However, West retains the ♥Q and drives out the ♠A for nine tricks and game.**

CHAPTER EIGHT

SLAM BIDDING   *THE ARTIFICAL 2♣ BID*   *BLACKWOOD*

Open 2♣: 22 + points or 8 1/2 playing tricks: 22 + HCP and length points.

The 2♣ bid is an artificial bid and shows 22+points and is <u>forcing</u> for one round of bidding. 8 1/2 playing tricks: Example: ♠AKQJ10654, ♥K10, ♦83, ♣10

2♦ response to 2♣ opening bid: Responder bids 2♦, an artificial <u>waiting</u> bid.

- Responder must respond 2♦, even with 0-points as partner has opened a 2♣ artificial bid.
- Responder's 2♦ bid keeps the bidding open to allow opener to bid his suit or 2NT.
- At his second turn to bid, responder can rebid 3♣ to show <u>0-3 points</u> over a major suit bid by his partner (3♦ serves the same purpose over a 3♣ rebid by opener).
- Responder can raise opener's suit, or respond to opener's 2NT with Stayman or notrump raises at his second turn to speak.
- Responder should usually not bid 2NT or 3NT as his first response.
- Responder can first bid his suit if holding three out of the top five honors in his 5+card suit, and at least eight points.

2NT opening bid: 20-21 points.

- Open <u>2NT</u> with <u>20-21 points</u> and a balanced hand, with no voids, no singletons, and at most, one doubleton. A 2NT bid by opener is not forcing. Responder can pass with a balanced hand and 0-4 points.
- Responder can bid Stayman at the three-level to ask partner to bid his four-card major.

Responder with no four-card major or 4-3-3-3- hand bid:
• 3NT - 5-10 points
• 6NT - 11-16 points
• 7NT - 17+points

Blackwood: 4NT artificial bid asking partner for aces and kings.

- When you bid a slam in a suit or notrump contract, you must know how many aces the partnership holds, as opponents with two aces can take the first two tricks by leading their aces, and you will make only 11 tricks, and not the 12 tricks required for a small slam. Do not ask for kings unless the partnership holds all four aces. The 5NT king-asking bid is a grand slam attempt. Blackwood is bid after a suit agreement. <u>With no suit agreement, the last suit bid naturally is considered to be the agreed trump suit.</u>

Blackwood: 4NT Artificial Bid.

4 NT Asks for Aces Responses	5NT Asks for Kings Responses
5♣ - 0 or 4 aces	6♣ - 0 or 4 kings
5♦ - 1 ace	6♦ - 1 king
5♥ - 2 aces	6♥ - 2 kings
5♠ - 3 aces	6♠ - 3 kings

#1 Sample Stayman and Blackwood hand over opener's rebid of 2NT:

West (Dealer)	2NT	3♣ (Stayman)	East	
♠AQJ2	3♠	4NT	♠K873	
♥AQ2	5♠ (three aces)	6♠ (small slam)		♥J653
♦A10	All Pass		♦KQ32	
♣K1098			♣A	

West opens 2NT with 20 points and a balanced hand.

- East bids 3♣, Stayman, asking partner for a four-card major. West bids 3♠ showing a four-card spade suit. East has a spade fit and 15 points (two extra points for the singleton ♣A with a spade fit). 15+20=35 points for small slam.
- East bids 4NT, Blackwood, asking partner for the number of aces in his hand. **Spades is the last suit bid naturally and considered the trump suit.**
- West bids 5♠ showing three aces. East bids the 6♠ small slam. Although holding all four aces, West's 2NT opening bid shows 20-21 points (21+ responder's 15=35). No need to look further for a grand slam, which requires 37- 40 points.
- After drawing trumps in three rounds, declarer finesses in hearts, throws one club on the diamond winner in dummy, and ruffs the other club in the dummy.

#2 Sample Blackwood hand: North and South pass throughout.

West (Dealer)			East
♠AKQJ	2♣	2♦ (waiting)	♠108
♥KQJ96	2♥	3♥ (invitational)	♥A432
♦A	4NT (Blackwood)	5♦ (one ace)	♦KQJ2
♣K43	6♥	All Pass	♣J103

West opens 2♣ with 24 points.

- East bids 2♦ (a waiting bid). West bids 2♥.
- With the heart fit, East now has 12 points (one point for the doubleton spade), and knows there is a combined partnership point count of at least 34 points for a small slam.
- **East bids 3♥, an invitational bid showing interest in slam. East would bid 4♥ with only enough points for game. The slower you go, the stronger your hand.**
- West bids 4NT (Blackwood), asking East for the number of aces in his hand.
- East bids 5♦ showing one ace. West missing only one ace, bids the 6♥ small slam.

#3 Sample Blackwood hand:

Contract: 6♠   West leads ♦10
Bidding:

South (Dealer)	West	North	East
2♣	Pass	2♦	Pass
2♠	Pass	3♠	Pass
4NT	Pass	5♦	Pass
6♠	All Pass		

North
♠J9732
♥KQ74
♦A7
♣Q10

West
♠4
♥A95
♦10964
♣76532

East
♠65
♥J108
♦8532
♣J984

South (Dealer)
♠AKQ108
♥632
♦KQJ
♣AK

- South bids 2♣ with 23 points.
- North with 13 points bids 2♦ (a waiting bid). South bids 2♠.
- North bids 3♠, slam invitational, as North could have bid 4♠ and closed the auction with only enough points for game.
- South bids 4NT - Blackwood, ace asking.
- North bids 5♦ (one ace). South missing only one ace, bids the 6♠ small slam.

The play: How to try to avoid two heart losers.

- South may a heart heart loser if East has the ♥A.
- Always lead toward double honors, in this case the ♥KQ in dummy.
- After drawing trumps, when South leads a small heart toward dummy, the ♥KQ will be winning tricks if West plays the ♥A.
- If West plays a low heart (not taking his ♥A), South will play the ♥K.
- Now South returns to his hand with the ♣A, and leads another heart toward the ♥Q in the dummy. South has finessed West for the ♥A.

CHAPTER EIGHT
THE BOTTOM LINE

SLAM REQUIREMENTS

Opener bids 2♣: **Artificial Bid**

22 or more points or 8 ½ Playing Tricks
- Opener rebids his longest suit or, rebids 2NT with a balanced hand.

Responder bids 2♦: **Artificial Bid**

- 2♦ a waiting bid by responder.
- At his second turn, responder rebids 3♣ to show 0-3 points over a major suit bid by his partner

Opener bids 2NT: **20-21 points - Balanced Hand**

Responses: No four card major or 4-3-3-3 hand
- 3NT - 5-10 points
- 6NT - 11-16 points
- 7NT – 17+points

BLACKWOOD:

---

4 NT Asks for Aces Responses	5NT Asks for Kings Responses
5♣ - 0 or 4 aces	6♣ - 0 or 4 kings
5♦ - 1 ace	6♦ - 1 king
5♥ - 2 aces	6♥ - 2 kings
5♠ - 3 aces	6♠ - 3 kings

- The Blackwood convention asks for the number of aces and kings held by your partnership. The 5NT king-asking bid is an attempt to bid a grand slam.
- Do not ask for kings unless the partnership holds all four aces.
- Blackwood is bid after a suit agreement, or with no suit agreement, the last suit bid naturally is considered to be the agreed trump suit.

#1   North
                                      ♠Q942
                                      ♥K10643
                                      ♦AK
                                      ♣A10

West   East
♠5   ♠63
♥752   ♥AJ
♦Q10754   ♦J9632
♣9873   ♣6542

                                      South (Dealer)
                                      ♠AKJ1087
                                      ♥Q98
                                      ♦8
                                      ♣KQJ

South is the dealer with _____points and bids_____; West passes; North with ____points bids____;
East passes; South bids____; West passes; North bids____; East passes; South bids____; West
passes; North bids____; All Pass. What is the contract____? Who is the declarer____? Who leads
the first card____? What is the lead___?

#2   North
                                      ♠AK32
                                      ♥J764
                                      ♦K1093
                                      ♣4

West   East
♠1098   ♠654
♥32   ♥Q95
♦J852   ♦74
♣Q1076   ♣KJ982

                                      South (Dealer)
                                      ♠QJ7
                                      ♥AK108
                                      ♦AQ6
                                      ♣A53

South is the dealer with _____points and bids ____; West passes; North with ____points bids____;
East passes; South bids____; West passes; North bids____; East passes; South bids____;
West passes; North bids ____; All Pass. What is the contract____? Who is the declarer____?
Who leads the first card____? What is the lead___?

#3

North (Dealer)
♠AK53
♥A63
♦AQ64
♣A10

West
♠J87
♥K95
♦J753
♣932

East
♠Q642
♥QJ102
♦98
♣J76

South
♠109
♥874
♦K102
♣KQ854

North is the dealer with _____points and bids ____; East passes; South with ____points bids____; All Pass. What is the contract____? Who is the declarer____? Who leads the first card____? What is the lead___?

#4

North
♠QJ83
♥KJ32
♦KQ62
♣10

West
♠74
♥84
♦10983
♣97642

East
♠10652
♥1076
♦J7
♣AJ53

South (Dealer)
♠AK9
♥AQ95
♦A54
♣KQ8

South is the dealer with _____points and bids _____; West passes; North with ____points bids____; East passes; South bids____; West passes; North bids____; East passes; South bids ____; West passes; North bids ____; East passes; South bids____; West passes; North bids____; All Pass. What is the contract____? Who is the declarer____? Who leads the first card____? What is the lead___?

#5

North
♠A74
♥Q862
♦93
♣AK73

West
♠J93
♥J1043
♦Q104
♣1085

East
♠10862
♥7
♦8652
♣QJ62

South (Dealer)
♠KQ5
♥AK95
♦AKJ7
♣94

South is the dealer and bids_____; West passes; North with _____points bids_____;
East passes; South bids____; West passes; North bids____; East passes; South bids _____; West
passes; North bids____; All Pass. What is the contract____? Who is the declarer____?
Who leads the first card____? What is the lead___?

#6

North (Dealer)
♠73
♥AJ96
♦A9
♣KQJ105

West
♠K1084
♥7
♦Q1064
♣8763

East
♠652
♥854
♦J8732
♣A72

South
♠AQJ9
♥KQ1032
♦K5
♣94

North is the dealer with ____points and bids____; East passes; South with ____points bids____;
West passes; North now with ____points bids____; East passes; South bids ____; West passes;
North bids____; East passes; South bids____; All Pass.What is the contract____?
Who is the declarer____? Who leads the first card____? What is the lead___?

#7   North (Dealer)
                                      ♠KJ73
                                      ♥AK
                                      ♦A84
                                      ♣AJ96
West   East
♠106   ♠842
♥Q9742   ♥J1086
♦J632   ♦1097
♣Q8   ♣1073
                                      South
                                      ♠AQ95
                                      ♥53
                                      ♦KQ5
                                      ♣K542

North is the dealer with ____points and bids____; East passes; South with ____points bids____;
West passes; North bids____; East passes; South bids____; West passes; North bids ____; East
passes; South bids____; North bids____; East passes; South bids___; All Pass. What is the
contract____? Who is the declarer____? Who leads the first card____? What is the lead___?

#8   North (Dealer)
                                      ♠AQJ
                                      ♥AKQ
                                      ♦AJ9
                                      ♣KJ109
West   East
♠6532   ♠1094
♥9874   ♥632
♦105   ♦876
♣732   ♣Q864
                                      South
                                      ♠K87
                                      ♥J105
                                      ♦KQ432
                                      ♣A5

North is the dealer with _____points and bids ____; East passes; South bids____; West passes;
North bids ____; East passes; South bids___; West passes: North bids____; East passes;
South bids____; West passes; North Bids ____; East passes; South bids____; All Pass.
What is the contract____? Who is the declarer____? Who leads the first card____?
What is the lead___?

120

#9

North
♠10743
♥Q9
♦1083
♣AJ73

West (Dealer)
♠A2
♥AKJ65
♦AKQ9
♣96

East
♠KJ65
♥10732
♦64
♣854

South
♠Q98
♥84
♦J752
♣KQ102

West is the dealer with _____points and bids____; North passes; East with _____points and bids____; South passes; West bids____; North passes; East bids____; All Pass. What is the contract____? Who is the declarer____? Who leads the first card____? What is the lead___?

#10

North (Dealer)
♠A1063
♥A43
♦53
♣J1096

West
♠J2
♥KQ8
♦AKJ
♣AKQ84

East
♠K8754
♥965
♦Q1087
♣7

South
♠Q9
♥J1072
♦9642
♣532

West is the dealer with _____points and bids ____; North passes; East ____points and bids ____; South passes; West bids ____; North passes; East bids____; South passes; West bids ____; All Pass. What is the contract____? Who is the declarer____? Who leads the first card____? What is the lead___?

Answers to practice hands on pages 116-120.

#1.
South is the dealer with 18 points and bids 1♠; West passes; North with 19 points (two points for doubleton diamonds and clubs with a spade fit) makes a forcing bid of 2♥; East passes; South jumps to 3♠ showing 16-18 points and a six+card spade suit; West passes; North bids 4NT (Blackwood). South bids 5♦ (one ace); North bids 6♠; All Pass. What is the contract? 6♠. Who is the declarer? South. Who leads the first card? West. What is the lead? ♣9- top of nothing.

- **North does not have to jump at his first bid to show the strength of his hand.**

- **A non-passed hand, North's bid of 2♥ is forcing opener must bid again.
  By making a forcing bid, North gets to learn more about partner's hand.**

- **South plans to show the strength of his hand at his rebid. South jumps to 3♠ showing 16-18 points and six spades. With no suit agreement, the last suit bid naturally is the agreed trump suit.**

- **South knows there may be a slam contract in spades and bids 4NT (Blackwood) to learn the number of aces in partner's hand. Missing only one ace, North bids 6♠. After drawing trumps, declarer will discard a heart loser on a top diamond, losing only one heart and making his ♠6 contract.**

#2
South is the dealer with 20 points and a balanced hand and bids 2NT; West passes; North with 11 points bids 3♣ (Stayman); East passes; South bids 3♥; West passes; North now with 13 points (two points for the singleton club with a heart fit) bids 4NT; East passes; South bids 5♠ (three aces); North bids 6♥; All Pass. What is the contract? 6♥. Who is the declarer? South. Who leads the first card? West. What is the lead? ♠10 - top of nothing lead.

- **When partner opens 2NT, North bids Stayman first to find a major fit.
  South bids 3♥, and North can re-evaluate his hand to 13 points with the singleton club.**

- **North bids 4NT (Blackwood) to learn the number of aces in partner's hand.**
- **South' 5♠ answer to Blackwood shows three aces. Although the partnership holds all four aces, South has limited his hand to 20-21 points by his opening 2NT bid. A grand slam does not seem to be an option with the combined 33 or 34-point count.**

- **The play involves early club ruffs in dummy. South wins in his hand with the ♠Q and plays the ♥A followed by the ♣A. South ruffs a club in dummy, and plays a low heart to the ♥10 in his hand, finessing East for the ♥Q. South ruffs a low club in dummy and draws the last trump, making the 6♥ contract.**

#3.

North is the dealer with 21 points and bids 2NT; East passes; South with 9 points bids 3NT; All Pass. What is the contract? 3NT. Who is the declarer? North. Who leads the first card? East. What is the lead? ♥Q - top of a three card sequence.

- **North's 2NT bid limited his hand to 21 points. The combined partnership points are not enough to explore for a slam, and South bids the 3NT game.**

- **South's club suit should be helpful to partner. With a good minor suit to run, it is usually better to playing a notrump contract than a five-level minor contract.**

#4 East and West pass throughout.
South is the dealer with 22 points and bids 2♣; North with 12 points bids 2♦ (waiting); South bids 2NT; North bids 3♣ (Stayman); South bids 3♥; North bids 4NT; East South bids 5♠ (three aces); North bids 6♥; All Pass. What is the contract? 6♥. Who is declarer? South. Who leads the first card? West. What is the lead? ♦10 - top of nothing lead.

- **North bids an artificial "waiting bid" of 2♦ to partner's 2♣ bids showing 22+points.**

- **South rebids 2NT, and North bids Stayman to learn if opener has a four-card major.**

- **South bids 3♥. Finding the heart fit, North can re-evaluate his hand to 14 point**
- **With the singleton club. North bids 4NT (Blackwood), to learn the number of aces in partner's hand.**

- **South 5♠ shows three aces. Missing only one ace, North bids the 6♥ slam.**

#5.

South is the dealer with 20 points and bids 2NT; North with 13 points bids 3♣;South bids 3♥; North bids 4NT; South bids 5♥ (two aces); North bids 6♥; All Pass. What is the contract? 6♥. Who is the declarer? South. Who leads the first card? West. What is the lead? ♣10 - a top of nothing.

- **South with 20 points opens 2NT; West passes; North with 13 points bids 3♣ (Stayman);**

- **South bids 3♥; with a heart fit, North bids 4NT (Blackwood), to learn the number of aces in partner's hand. South bids 5♥, showing two aces. North bids 6♥.**

- **Although holding four aces, a grand slam seems unlikely, as partner did not open 2♣.South will trump two diamond losers in dummy, and only lose the ♥J making the 6♥ slam.**

#6

North is the dealer with 16 points and bids 1♣; East passes; South with 16 points bids 1♥; North now with 18 points jumps to 3♥; South bids 4NT; North bids 5♥; East passes; South bids 6♥; All Pass. What is the contract? 6♥. Who is the declarer? South. Who leads the first card? West. What is the lead? ♣8 - top of nothing lead.

- **A NPH South makes a forcing bid of a new suit by bidding 1♥.**

- **With the heart fit, North jumps to 3♥ (18 points), counting two points for the spade and diamond doubletons. South re-evaluates his hand to 18 points, counting two points for the diamond and club doubletons. South counts enough points for a small slam, and bids 4NT to learn the number of partner's aces.**

- **North bids 5♥ to show two aces and, missing only one ace, South bids the 6♥ slam.**

- **West does not want to lead low from ♠K honor in his hand, as when the opponents are in a slam contract, it's usually best to make a safe top of nothing lead. South draw trumps.**

- **North does not play diamonds as he must leave the ♦A in dummy as an entry card to dummy's club suit.**

- **North plays on clubs, East wins the second round of the suit, and leads a Spade - the weak suit in the dummy.**

- **South forgoes a finesse of the ♠K and plays the ♠A, knowing he can enter dummy with the ♦A to sluff losing spades on the good clubs in dummy.**

#7.

North is the dealer with 20 points and bids 2NT; East passes; South with 14 points bids 3♣ (Stayman); West passes; North bids 3♠; East passes; South now with 15 points bids 4NT; West passes; North bids 5♠; East passes; South bids 5NT (having all the aces asks for kings); North bids 6♥ (two kings); South bids 7♠; All Pass. What is the contract? 7♠. Who is the declarer? North. Who leads the first card? East.

What is the lead? ♥J.

- **After North's 2NT opening bid, South bids Stayman asking partner for his four-card major. Hearing the spade fit, South adds one point for the heart doubleton, now holding 15 points.**

- **South bids 4NT (Blackwood) asking North for his number of aces; North's 5♠ bid shows three aces. South knows the partnership holds four aces, and bids 5NT to ask partner for his number of kings. North's 6♥ bid shows two kings. Holding four aces and four kings, South bids the 7♠ grand slam. The contract can also make 7NT.**

#8

North is the dealer with 25 points and bids 2♣; South with 14 points bids 2♦; North with **game in hand jumps to 3NT showing 25-26 points**; South bids 4NT; North bids 5♠; South bids 5NT; North bids 6♥; South bids 7NT; All Pass. What is the contract? 7NT. Who is the declarer? North. Who leads the first card? East. What is the lead? ♠10.

- **North's jump to 3NT game after opening 2♣ showing a "game in hand" point count of 25-26+points. South counts North's 25 minimum points to his 14 points and knows there may be a grand slam.**

- **South bids 4NT asking partner for his number of aces. North's 5♠ bid shows three aces. South bids 5NT asking partner for his number of kings. North's 6♥ bid shows two kings. The partnership holds four aces and four kings and at least 39 points.**

- **South bids the 7NT grand slam.**

#9 East and West pass throughout.

West is the dealer with 22 points and bids 2♣; West bids 2♦; West bids 2♥; East bids 4♥; All Pass. What is the contract? 4♥; Who is the declarer? West; Who leads the first card? North. What is the lead? ♦10 top of nothing.

- **East with a minimum hand, closes the contract by bidding 4♥.**

- **West will play the ♥AK holding a nine-card trump fit, hoping to drop the ♥Q.**

#10 North and South pass throughout.

West is the dealer with 24 points bids 2♣; North passes; East with 6 points bids 2♦; South passes; West bids 3♣; North passes; East bids 3♠; South passes; West bids 3NT; All Pass. What is the contract? 3NT. Who is the declarer? West. Who leads the first card? North. What is the lead? ♠3.

- **South's ♠Q wins the opening lead, and he returns the suit. Declarer's ♠J forces North's ♠A. Declarer will play the ♥K to set up the 9th trick. North wins leading ♣J.**

- **Declarer wins in hand, and plays the ♦AKJ, overtaking the ♦J with the ♦Q in dummy, making his contract with one spade, one heart, four diamonds, and three clubs.**

NOTES

 **CHAPTER NINE**

SCORING THE GAME   QUIZZES   OVERVIEW

Duplicate or Chicago Style scoring are outlined in this chapter. Although based on Rubber Bridge, duplicate and Chicago scoring are more in use today than Rubber Bridge scoring.

 **GAME AND SLAM BONUS POINTS**

Non-Vulnerable Bonus Points		**Vulnerable Bonus Points**	
Part Score	50 points	Part Score	50 points
Game	300 points	Game	500 points
Small Slam	500 points	Small Slam	750 points
Grand Slam	1000 points	Grand Slam	1500 points

Trick Points

> ♠Spades = 30 points per trick
>
> ♥Hearts = 30 points per trick
>
> ♦Diamonds = 20 points per trick
>
> ♣Clubs = 20 points per trick
>
> No Trump = 40 points for first trick, 30 points for each additional trick

The scoring below describes major suit games and small slams. Adjust per trick scores for games and slams in the minor suits, notrump contracts and bonus points for grand slams.

Add bonus points plus per trick points for game and slams:

Game points: Add game bonus points+per trick points to arrive a game scores.

Non-vulnerable game: 300 bonus points+4 tricks x 30 points = 120 points = 420 total points.
Vulnerable game: 500 bonus points+4 tricks x 30 points = 120 points = 620 total points.

Slam points: Game bonus points+slam bonus points+per trick points = slam scores.

Non-vulnerable small slam: 500 slam bonus points+300 game bonus points+ 6 trick
Total points = 980 for non-vulnerable small slam

Vulnerable small slam: 750 slam bonus points+500 game bonus points+6 tricks
Total points = 1430 for vulnerable small slam.

Part Score Points

- Part scores are bids below games or slam contracts. When your partnership declares the contract but does not have the required points to bid game, you will "settle" for a part score.

- Vulnerability is not a factor in making part scores. You make the same 50 bonus points + per trick points.

- You only make extra bonus points when you bid and make a games or slams.

Example:

- You bid 3♠ and you make 4♠ ten tricks, in other words or an "overtrick". You receive the 50 bonus points for the part score, and per trick points of 30 points per trick x 4 = 120 +50 bonus points for a total score of 170 points.

- If you bid a 4♠ game, you would receive an additional 300 bonus points for a non-vulnerable game, and have a score of 420 points. 300+120 = 420

You get <u>50 bonus points</u> plus per trick points for making part scores.

Spade and heart part scores - 1, 2 or 3 ♠/♥

1♠/1♥ = 30 for 1 trick+50 bonus part score = 80 points
2♠/2♥ = 60 for 2 tricks+50 bonus part score = 110 points
3♠/3♥ = 90 for 3 tricks+50 bonus part score = 140 points

Diamond and club part scores - 1, 2, 3, or 4 ♦/♣

1♦/1♣ = 20 for 1 trick+ 50 bonus part score = 70 points
2♦/2♣ = 40 for 2 tricks+50 bonus part score = 90 points
3♦/3♣ = 60 for 3 tricks+50 onus part score = 110 points
4♦/4♣ = 80 for 4 tricks+50 bonus part score = 130 points

1NT or 2NT

1NT = 40 for first trick +50 bonus part score = 90 points
2NT = 70 for 2 tricks+50 bonus part score = 120 points

Vulnerability is a factor when you go down tricks or don't make your contract.

- In a non-vulnerable contract you lose 50 points for every trick you go down, and in a vulnerable contract you lose 100 points for every trick you go down.

Penalties for going down in a doubled contract.

A defender may double your contract if he thinks you will not make the contract.

- Non-vulnerable game: doubled: Down-1 = 100; 2 = 300; 3 = 500; 4 = 800; -5 = 1100
  Vulnerable game: doubled: Down-1 = 200; 2 = 500; 3 = 800; 4 = 1100 etc.

How many points did you win in the contracts?   Answers at bottom of page

V IS FOR VULNERABLE   NV IS FOR NON-VULNERABLE

#1   3♠_____   2♠_____   1♠_____   V 4♠_____

#2   1♥_____   V 6♥_____   V 4♥_____   3♥_____

#3   V 5♦_____   3♦_____   2♦_____   NV 6♦_____

#4   V 3NT_____   2NT_____   1NT_____   V 5NT_____

#5   NV 6NT_____   V7 NT_____   V 7♠_____   NV 7♣_____

#6   NV 5♦_____   4♦_____   2♥_____   V 6♦_____

Answers: How many points did you win in the contracts?

#				
#1	3♠ - 140	2♠ - 110	1♠ - 80	V 4♠ - 620
#2	1♥ - 80	V 6♥ - 1430	V 4♥ - 620	3♥ - 140
#3	V 5♦ - 600	3♦ - 110	2♦ - 90	NV 6♦ - 920
#4	V 3NT - 600	2NT - 120	1NT - 90	V 5NT - 660
#5	NV 6NT - 990	V 7NT - 2220	V 7♠ - 2210	NV 7♣ - 1440
#6	NV 5♦ - 400	`4♦ - 130	2♥ - 110	V 6♦ - 1370

How many points did you win or lose?   Answers bottom of page.

X - Doubled Contract   Vulnerable - V   Non-vulnerable - NV

Contract: 4♠ X V – you only made 3: How many points to opponents_____?

Contract: 2♠ – you made 3: how many points to you_____?

Contract: 3NT V – you made 3: how many points to you_____?

Contract: 4 ♥ NV – you only made 2: how many points to opponents_____?

Contract: 5♦ NV – you made 4: how many points to opponents_____?

Contract: 2♣ – you made 2: how many points to you_____?

Contract: 4♥ V – you made 4: how many points to you_____?

Contract: 6♠ V – you made 6: how many points to you_____?

Contract: 4♠ X V – you only made 3: how many points to opponents_____?

Contract: 2NT V – you made 3: how many points to you_____?

 Answers: How many points did you win or lose in the following contracts?

Contract: 4♠ X V – you only made 3, down one doubled: 200 points to opponents.

Contract: 2♠ – you made 3, an overtrick: 140 points to you.

Contract: 3NT V – you made 3: 600 points to you for vulnerable 3NT game.

Contract: 4♥ NV – you only made 2, down 2 NV: 100 points to opponents.

Contract: 5♦ NV – you only made 4, down one NV: 50 points to opponents.

Contract: 2♣ – you made 2: 90 points to you.

Contract: 4♥ V – you made 4: 620 points to you for vulnerable 4♥ game.

Contract: 6♠ V – you made 6: 1430 points to you for vulnerable small slam.

Contract: 4♠ X V – you only made 3, down one vulnerable: 200 points to opponents.

Contract: 2NT V – you made 3: 150 points to you for part score.

Do you bid a game or part score?   Answers for #3 - #9 on pages 133 - 134.

D= Doubleton; S = Singleton; V = Void; Resp = Responder; PT SC = Part Score
#1 and #2 are sample hands with answers.

OPENER	BID	BID	RESP	GAME	PT SC
♠KQ1098	1♠	2♠	♠543	4♠	
♥K52	3♠	4♠	♥QJ76		
♦AK6			♦43		
♣32			♣KQ54		
Points = 16	17+1 D♣		Points = 9 +1 D♦		

#2

OPENER	BID	BID	RESP	GAME	PT SC
♠A2	1♥	1NT	♠543	4♥	
♥KQ5432	3♥	4♥	♥A6		
♦Q76			♦K10432		
♣A6			♣Q54		
Points = 17			Points = 10		

#3

OPENER	BID	BID	RESP	GAME	PT SC
♠J109			♠52		
♥AQ765			♥8432		
♦1098			♦QJ43		
♣A2			♣KQ5		
Points =			Points =		

#4

OPENER	BID	BID	RESP	GAME	PT SC
♠AQ98			♠1076		
♥Q1075			♥10432		
♦42			♦AK2		
♣AJ2			♣1098		
Points =			Points =		

#5

OPENER	BID	BID	RESP	GAME	PT SC
♠KQ1098			♠J42		
♥AKJ2			♥76		
♦32			♦AJ76		
♣A8			♣J432		
Points =			Points =		

#6

OPENER	BID	BID	RESP	GAME	PT SC
♠KJ1082			♠Q6		
♥KJ10			♥Q92		
♦A32			♦K765		
♣J10			♣Q743		
Points =			Points =		

#7

OPENER	BID	BID	RESP	GAME	PT SC
♠KJ10964			♠A2		
♥5			♥A9		
♦A65			♦K10982		
♣K65			♣J1098		
Points =			Points =		

#8

OPENER	BID	BID	RESP	GAME	PT SC
♠AJ10			♠KQ32		
♥AJ86			♥KJ5		
♦863			♦J109		
♣KQ4			♣632		
Points =			Points =		

#9

OPENER	BID	BID	RESP	GAME	PT SC
♠652			♠QJ4		
♥AJ92			♥KQ76		
♦KJ103			♦Q54		
♣AK			♣642		
Points =			Points =		

Do you bid game or part score (Part Sc)? Answers for quiz on pages 131 - 132.

#3

OPENER	BID	BID	RESP	GAME	PT SC
♠J109	1♥	2♥	♠52		2♥
♥AQ765	Pass		♥8432		
♦1098			♦QJ43		
♣A2			♣KQ5		
Points = 12			Points = 9 1 points D♠		

#4

OPENER	BID	BID	RESP	GAME	PT SC
♠AQ98	1♣	1♥	♠1076		2♥
♥Q1075	2♥	Pass	♥10432		
♦42			♦AK2		
♣AJ2			♣1098		
Points = 13			Points = 7		

#5

OPENER	BID	BID	RESP	GAME	PT SC
♠KQ1098	1♠	2♠	♠J42	4♠	
♥AKJ2	4♠	Pass	♥76		
♦32			♦AJ76		
♣A8			♣J432		
Points = 18	20 points 2 D ♦ ♣		Points = 8	1 point for D♥	

#6

OPENER	BID	BID	RESP	GAME	PT SC
♠KJ1082	1♠	1NT	♠Q6		1NT
♥KJ10	Pass		♥Q92		
♦A32			♦K765		
♣J10			♣Q743		
Points = 14			Points = 9		

#7

OPENER	BID	BID	RESP	GAME	PT SC
♠KJ10964	1♠	2♦	♠A2	4♠	
♥5	2♠	4♠	♥A9		
♦A65	Pass		♦K10982		
♣K65			♣J1098		
Points = 13	Six-card spade		Points = 13	14 points 1 D♥	

#8

OPENER	BID	BID	RESP	GAME	PT SC
♠AJ10	1NT	2♣ Stayman	♠KQ32	3NT	
♥AJ86	2♥	3NT	♥KJ5		
♦863	Pass		♦J109		
♣KQ4			♣632		
Points = 15			Points = 10		

#9

OPENER	BID	BID	RESP	GAME	PT SC
♠652	1NT	2♣ Stayman	♠QJ4	4♥	
♥AJ92	2♥	4♥	♥KQ76		
♦KJ103	Pass		♦Q54		
♣AK			♣642		
Points = 16			Points = 10		

OPENER BIDS	SUITS	POINTS
One of a major suit.	Five+card suit.	12+points
One of a minor suit.	Three+card suit, may have no five+card major.	12+points
One notrump.	Balanced hand, no singletons, no voids, only one doubleton.	15-17 HCP
Open one of a major, and then jump in the major.	Six+card suit.	16-18 points
Open one of a major, then jump shift into new suit.	May be three+card suit.	19-21 points
Open one in a suit, jump to 2NT.	Balanced hand.	18-21 points
RESPONDER BIDS **_WITH_ SUPPORT** Raise at the two-level.	Three+card support for partner, **non-forcing.**	6-10 points
Limit raise, jump to the three-level.	Three+card suit, **non-forcing (prefer four+card suit w/10).**	10-12 points
Bid new suit at the two-level; partner does not jump or support your suit, rebid game in opener's major suit.	Bid new suit, *forcing (NPH).*	13-16 points
With 4+card suit plus support for partner.	Bid new suit, *forcing (NPH),* then support partner. May explore for slam.	17+points

RESPONDER BIDS **_WITHOUT_ SUPPORT**	**SUITS**	**POINTS**
Bid 1NT	May be unbalanced hand with no other bid.	6-10 points
Bid 2NT.	Balanced hand.	11-12 points
Bid 3NT.	Balanced hand.	13-15 points
Bid new suit at one-level. Rebid jump in six+card suit to invite game.	five+card suit.	6+ points 11-12 points
Bid new suit at two-level.	Over 1♠, five+card heart suit or two-level four+card minor suit; *forcing* by a NPH.	10+points
Bid suit, then jump in suit. Make a forcing bid and may explore for slam.	Six+card suit.	11-12 points - invite 17+points

NOTES

ADDENDUM

AMERICAN CONTRACT BRIDGE LEAGUE

STYLES OF BRIDGE GAMES

American Contract Bridge League:

The American Contract Bridge League (ACBL) was founded in 1937, and celebrated its 75th birthday in 2012. ACBL is the largest Bridge organization in the world with over 160,000 members in the United States, Canada, Mexico and Bermuda.

The ACBL is a non-profit organization, dealing with the rules of Bridge, education, and Sanctioned clubs and tournament games. You can contact ACBL to find duplicate games in your area. ACBL'S website is www.acbl.org; toll free telephone number 800-467-1623.

Styles of Bridge Games: Duplicate, Rubber and Chicago Style Bridge

The scoring used in duplicate and Chicago Bridge derives from Rubber Bridge scoring as did the terms vulnerable contracts and non-vulnerable contracts.

Rubber Bridge:

- In Rubber Bridge scoring, the first game your side scores earns non-vulnerable bonus points.

- When you or your opponents score a "game on," that pair becomes vulnerable. The pair with no game is non-vulnerable.

- When you are vulnerable, you win more bonus points when you make games, and lose more points when your game or part score fails to make.

- If you win two games before the opponents can win two games, you win the "rubber" and added bonus points. In Rubber Bridge, extra points are also given for honor cards in trump suits.

- When a pair has a part score (partial) in Rubber Bridge, they need only make additional part scores to create a game score.

- This method of scoring left many hands bid only to partial games with game going points. Many hands were underbid, as only partials were needed to win the rubber.

- Today, duplicate and Chicago style Bridge are more popular than Rubber Bridge, as most players prefer the challenge of bidding to the maximum level of their combined point count.

Chicago Bridge:

- Chicago Style Bridge is often used in home games. Players draw for the high card to see who will deal first. The deal proceeds clockwise around the table after each deal.

- No one is vulnerable on the first deal. On the second and third deals, the dealer's side is vulnerable, and on the last deal, both side are vulnerable. Each rubber consists of only four deals before the partnerships change.

Duplicate Bridge:

- Duplicate Bridge is played throughout the world. Virtually every locale has one or more duplicate Bridge clubs, and there are hundreds of tournaments played yearly throughout the United States and internationally.

- In addition, computer online duplicate games can be played any time of the day or night. Bridgebase Online is a popular site for on-line Bridge. www.bridgebaseonline.com.

- Duplicate play is considered an equitable form of Bridge, as winning does not merely rely on holding high cards. Good defense is equally important to winning the game. It is how you score relative to everyone else holding the very same cards as you -- since each deal is played many times during the Bridge session, and the cards preserved in a specially constructed board.

Duplicate play:

- Duplicate Bridge games are arranged as numbered tables where partnerships play in positions of either North-South or East-West.

- Cards are placed in "boards" (card holders) and, after the hand has been played, the boards are passed to the next lowered numbered table in the Mitchell movement.

- The Mitchell movement is one type of duplicate play. When the boards are passed to lower tables at completion of a round, the East-West players move to the next higher table -- and so on after each round.

- The North-South players usually remain stationary at their opening tables. The boards and East-West players continue to move until all of the boards are played

- A director runs the game, and inputs all the scores into a manual score sheet or an ACBL computer program, which calculates the percentage points for each pair on each deal and overall for the whole event. The North-South pairs compete against each other, which also applies for the East-West pairs. The pairs in each direction with the highest scores win the duplicate session. Duplicate Bridge is usually played in duplicate clubs, and can also be played in home games with two or more tables in play.

# GLOSSARY

American Contract Bridge League (ACBL): ACBL is non-profit organization dealing with the rules of Bridge, Bridge education, sanctioned clubs and tournament games.

Artificial bid: A bid that may convey a different or additional meaning than the actual bid made.

Auction: A Bridge auction is the calling of bids by players clockwise around the table until a final contract is reached.

Balanced hand: A Bridge hand with even distribution of cards throughout the suits. It will not contain a void or singleton or more than one doubleton.

Bid: The naming of a suit, notrump or pass.

Blackwood convention: A 4NT bid asking partner for the number of aces and kings in his hand.

Book: The first six tricks taken by declarer.

Call: A double, redouble or pass.

Contract: The final bid in the auction followed by three passes.

Convention: A partnership agreement that allocates a specific meaning to a bid in terms of the suit held or the strength of the hand.

Cover: A play of attempting to beat an opponent's honor with your honor in the attempt to win the trick, or to set-up a lower honor in your hand or partner's hand as a subsequent winner.

Discard: Playing a card from another suit when void in the suit led.

Doubleton: An original holding consisting of only two cards in a suit.

Finesse: The finesse is a form of declarer play of attempting to capture a an opponent's honor between lower and higher honors.

Fit: The partnership looks for an "Ideal Fit" of 8+cards in any one suit.

Follow suit: Players must always follow to the suit led.

Forcing: A bid that forces partner to bid for at least one more round of bidding.

Invitational bid: A bid that invites partner to bid game, but does not compel him to do so.

Jump bid: A bid that raises the bidding by one or more levels than is necessary. So a raise from one heart to two hearts is not a jump, but a bid of three hearts over one heart would be a jump level.

Jump shift: A bid that skips a level of bidding, and shifts to another suit in the jump bid than the suit previously called.

Loser: A card that will surrender a trick to the opponents.

Part score: Contracts below game levels.

Pass: No call

Penalty: Points assigned to the defending team when a contract fails.

Point count: Players use the Framework of Bidding to evaluate the points in their hands.

Quick tricks (QT): Aces, Aces with kings or queens, kings with small cards.

Rebid: Subsequent bids by opener or responder after their initial call.

Re-evaluation: Recounting the points in your hand due to information gained in the bidding.

Ruff: Use to a trump card to win a trick when void in the suit led.

Ruff and sluff: The ability to trump or ruff a card in one hand, and throw away a losing card in the other hand. Both hands must be void in the suit led for a ruff and sluff to apply. Also called a ruff and discard.

Sequence: Two or more contiguous cards in a suit.

Set: Defeating the contract.

Singleton: A holding of only one card in a suit.

Spot card: Cards below the jack in any suit.

Stayman convention: An artificial 2♣ bid over a 1NT opening bid, or a 3♣ bid over a 2NT opening bid, asking the notrump opener for a four-card major.

Support: The concept of raising the level of partner's suit.

Trick: The clockwise play of four cards, a single card from each of the four players to make up a unit of four cards.

Trump: The suit named by a partnership in the final contract.

Void: Holding no cards in a suit.

Vulnerability: An artificially assigned state of the contract in Duplicate and Chicago scoring. There are higher scores for vulnerable successful contracts then for non-vulnerable contracts, and penalties are increased for failed vulnerable contracts.

5+CARD MAJOR BIDDING SYSTEM:

High card points (HCP) for honor cards: ACE = 4; KING = 3; QUEEN = 2; JACK = 1;

LENGTH POINTS: COUNT ONE POINT FOR EACH CARD OVER 4 CARDS IN A SUIT.

OPENING BIDS.

Open with a good 12+points and five+cards in a major suit.

No 5+card major, open a 3+cards minor; Open 1♦ with 4♦; open 1♣ with 3-3 minor cards.

RESPONDER:

RESPONDER MUST BID WITH 6+POINTS; PASS WITH 0-5 POINTS.

A NEW SUIT BY NON-PASSED (NPH) RESPONDER IS *FORCING* FOR ONE MORE ROUND.

RAISE OF PARTNER'S SUIT OR NT BIDS ARE <u>NOT NEW SUITS AND NOT FORCING.</u>

RESPONDER'S OPTIONS WITH SUPPORT FOR PARTNER'S SUIT.

OPTION #1: (6-10) points: **SIMPLE <u>RAISE</u>**   Three+cards in partner's suit – bid at two-level .

OPTION #2: (10-12) points: **LIMIT RAISE**   Three +cards in partner's suit – jump to three-level.

OPTION #3: 13-15 points: Bid new suit at one or two-level, then with 13-15 points, bid game in partner's suit after partner's non-jump rebid.

OPTION #4: 16+ points: Make a forcing bid and explore for slam.

RESPONDER'S OPTIONS *WITHOUT* SUPPORT FOR PARTNER'S SUIT.

OPTION #5: 6-11 points: A PH responder bids a new suit or notrump at one-level. With 10-11 points bids a 5+ hearts over a 1♠ or any two-level 4+card minor. Responder's jump rebid in his suit shows a six+card suit 11-12 points - invitational.

OPTION #6: 6+points: A NPH responder's one-level bid of new suit is forcing, non-forcing by PH.

OPTION #7: 10-16 points: Bid new five+card heart suit or any four+card minor suit at the two-level, then jump in your suit with six+cards and 11-12 points, invitational. Non-forcing by PH.

OPTION #8 17+ points: May jump shift on your rebid. Slam invitational.

RESPONDER'S OPTIONS WHEN PARTNER OPENS A MINOR SUIT.

OPTION #9: 6+points: Over opener's minor opening, bid four-card majors up the line. With no 4+card major, and 5+cards in opener's minor, responder can raise suit to the two-level, or limit raise to the three-level. NPH forcing or PH non-forcing.

RESPONDER'S NOTRUMP BIDS: BALANCED HANDS – NO SUPPORT FOR PARTNER

OPTION #10: 6-10 POINTS BID 1NT; 11-12 POINTS BID 2NT; 13-15 POINTS BID 3NT

REBIDS BY OPENER AND RESPONDER: (spades sample suit).

Responder with support for Opener

OPENER	RESPONDER At least 3+cards in the suit
1♠	2♠ Simple raise 6-10 points: LOW
1♠	3♠ Jump to three-level: LIMIT RAISE10-12 points: MEDIUM
1♠	Make a forcing new suit at the two-level, the rebid game after non-jump bid by opener and explore for slam. 16+POINTS: HIGH

Opener's rebid hearing support from partner:

OPENER	RESPONDER	OPENER
1♠	2♠	12-15 POINTS: PASS: LOW
		3♠ 16-18 POINTS INVITE GAME: MEDIUM
		4♠ BID GAME: 19-21 POINTS: HIGH

Opener with support with support for partner At least 4+cards in the suit.

OPENER	RESPONDER	OPENER
1♥	1♠	2♠ 12-15 POINTS: LOW
1♥	1♠	3♠ 16-18 POINTS INVITE GAME: MEDIUM
1♥	1♠	4♠ BID GAME: 19-21 POINTS: HIGH

OPENER'S JUMP SHIFT SHOWS 19-21 POINTS AND IS FORCING TO GAME.

TRUMP SUIT: "IDEAL" EIGHT+CARD FIT WITH PARTNER.

SHORT SUITS: Count short suits points only when you have found an eight+card fit with partner.

Short suit points: <u>Declarer:</u> Singletons - 1 card in a suit = 2 points; doubletons - 2 cards in a suit = 1 point; Void - 0 cards in a suit = 3 points.

Responder: Singletons - 1 card in a suit = 2 points; doubletons - 2 cards in a suit = 1 point; Void - 0 cards in a suit = to the number of dummy's trumps.

NO TRUMP OPENING. 15-17 High Card Points

NO SINGLETONS - NO VOIDS - ONLY ONE DOUBLETON.

STAYMEN RESPONSE TO OPENING 1NT OR 2NT.

2♣/3♣: ARTIFICIAL 2♣/3♣ BID BY RESPONDER ASKS FOR FOUR-CARD MAJOR. OPENER BIDS FOUR-CARD MAJORS UP THE LINE HOLDING BOTH MAJORS.

2♦. BID BY NO TRUMP OPENER DENIES A FOUR-CARD MAJOR.

RESPONDER'S REBID AFTER OPENER'S RESPONSE.

8-9 POINTS: BID 2NT WITH <u>NO FIT</u> IN THE MAJOR

10-14 POINTS: BID 3NT WITH <u>NO FIT</u> IN THE MAJOR

8-9 POINTS: <u>WITH A FIT</u> IN THE MAJOR, BID THREE OF THE MAJOR TO INVITE OPENER TO GAME.

10-14 POINTS: <u>WITH A FIT</u> IN THE MAJOR, BID GAME IN MAJOR

OPENER	DISTRIBUTION	POINTS
1NT	BALANCED HAND - NO VOIDS NO SINGLETONS ONLY ONE DOUBLETON	15-17 POINTS
RESPONDER	STAYMAN ASKS OPENER FOR FOUR-CARD MAJOR	8+POINTS
2NT	NO FOUR-CARD MAJOR INVITATION TO 3NT GAME	9 POINTS
3NT	BID 3NT GAME	10-14 POINTS

2♣ ARTIFICAL STRONG HAND: 22+POINTS.

2♣ OPENER - 22+ POINTS - ARTIFICIAL BID

2♦ RESPONDER - 0 + POINTS - ARTIFICIAL WAITING BID

2 NT OPENER - 20-21 POINTS AND BALANCED DISTRIBUTION.

RESPONDER'S BIDS TO OPENING 2NT

5+ POINTS: BID STAYMAN WITH FOUR-CARD MAJOR.

5-10 POINTS: BID 3NT WITH BALANCED HAND.

12+ POINTS: BID BLACKWOOD – ASKING NUMBER OF ACES.

SLAM BIDDING.

<u>BID 4NT - BLACKWOOD CONVENTION ACE/KING ASK;</u>

<u>WITH ALL 4 ACES - 5NT ASKS FOR KINGS</u>

RESPONSE	RESPONSE
5♣ - 0 OR 4 ACES	6♣ - 0 OR 4 KINGS
5♦ - 1 ACE	6♦ - 1 KING
5♥ - 2 ACES	6♥ - 2 KINGS
5♠ - 3 ACES	6♠ - 3 KINGS

PARTNERSHIP POINTS NEEDED FOR GAME AND SLAM CONTRACTS.

3NT	GAME IN NO TRUMP	25 – 26 POINTS
4♠/4♥	GAME IN THE MAJORS	25 – 26 POINTS
5♦/5♣	GAME IN THE MINORS	27 – 29 POINTS
6NT/6♠/6♥/6♦/6♣	SMALL SLAM	33 -36 POINTS
7NT/7♠/7♥/7♦/7♣	GRAND SLAM	37 - 40 POINTS

6-15-2019

Made in the USA
Lexington, KY
14 December 2019